LOOKING INTO CLASSROOMS: PAPERS ON DIDACTICS

Issues in Curriculum Theory, Policy, and Research

Ian Westbury and Margery Osborne, Series Editors

Deliberation in Education and Society
    edited by J. T. Dillon, 1994

The Pursuit of Curriculum: Schooling and the Public Interest
    by William A. Reid, 1994

In Search of More Effective Mathematics Education: Examining Data for the IEA Second International Mathematics Study
    edited by Ian Westbury, Corinna A. Ethington, Lauren A. Sosniak, and David P. Baker, 1994

Reconceiving Mathematics Instruction: A Focus on Errors
    by Raffaella Borasi, 1996

Looking into Classrooms: Papers on Didactics
    by Peter Menck, 2000

Against the Odds: The Meaning of School and Relationships in the Lives of Six Young African-American Men
    by Jeremy Nicholas Price, 2000

LOOKING INTO CLASSROOMS: PAPERS ON DIDACTICS

by
Peter Menck
Universität Gesamthochschule-Siegen

Introduction by
Ian Westbury
University of Illinois at Urbana-Champagne

Ablex Publishing Corporation
Stamford, Connecticut

Copyright © 2000 by Ablex Publishing Corporation

Printed in the United States of America

Library of Congress Cataloging-in-Publication Data

Menck, Peter.
    Looking into classrooms: papers on didactics / by Peter Menck.
        p.   cm. — (Issues in curriculum theory, policy, and research)
    Includes bibliographical references and index.
    ISBN 1-56750-484-1 (cloth)—ISBN 1-56750-468-x (pbk.)
    1. Teaching—Philosophy. 2. Education—Philosophy. 3.Personality development. I. Title. II. Series.
  LB1025.3.M47 2000
  371.102′01 21—dc21   99-045874
                                              CIP

Ablex Publishing Corporation
100 Prospect Street
P.O. Box 811
Stamford, CT 06904-0811

Contents

Acknowledgments vii

Introduction by Ian Westbury. xi

Chapter 1. Research in Education and Didactics in Germany. 1

Chapter 2. *Bildung:* A Core Concept of German Didaktik 11

Chapter 3. General Didactics: A Theoretical Framework 19

Chapter 4. Can We (and What Can We) Learn from the
              History of Education? 41

Chapter 5. Content: Still in Question?. 55

Chapter 6. Didactics As Construction of Content 71

Chapter 7. Throwing Dice: The Content of a Math Lesson 87

Chapter 8. The Formation of Conscience: A Lost Topic of Didaktik 95

Chapter 9. *Bild, Bildung, Weltbild.* 111

Notes. 125

References 131

Author Index. 137

Subject Index 139

Acknowledgments

It is quite unusual for a German educationist to write a book in English and this book would never have been possible without the substantial help of many people. I need to thank them all.

It was the members of the "Didaktik meets Curriculum" group who first encouraged me to work out my ideas in English: Sigrun Gudmundsdottir (Norwegian University of Science and Technology, Trondheim, Norway), Börg B. Gundem (University of Oslo, Norway), Stefan Hopmann (Norwegian University of Science and Technology, Trondheim, Norway), Rudolf Künzli (Didaktikum, Aarau, Switzerland), Roland Lauterbach (University of Dresden, Germany), Kurt Riquarts (Institute for Science Education—IPN—at the University of Kiel, Germany), and Ian Westbury (University of Illinois at Urbana-Champaign, USA). The discussions of the group at the meetings at Aarau, Kiel, Oslo, and at the American Educational Research Association (AERA) meetings at New Orleans and Chicago, opened up something like a second career for me.

This invitation to think something new was strongly supported by two visits to the Stockholm Institute of Education. Gert Arfvedson, Björn Falkevall, Gull-Britt Larsson, and Ingemar Nilsson, and Gerd Arfvedson above all, gave me another opportunity to test whether or not colleagues outside my tradition involved in teacher training could make use of some of my issues. And at all of these meetings and seminars on two continents it was not only "Didaktik or Curriculum": The persons with whom I talked about educational research made me feel at home wherever I was.

My English studies date from the early 1950s when I was a student in a German *Gymnasium*. I had not made much use of them until 1991 when I first attended a "Didaktik meets Curriculum" meeting. I was therefore very grateful that I found translators who mastered the two-part task I gave them of understanding what I wanted to say in German and translating it into English: Gilian Horton-Krüger who was then at the IPN in Kiel, and Stefanie Pirags, Annette Jungmann, Alexandra Dommes, Ilse Runkel, and Jutta Linsel, all students of the University of Siegen. These "translators" helped me see my former thinking and writing in a different light: On the one hand, some problems turned out to be nothing but specific German quarrels; on the other hand, arguments that seemed to be clear asked for further elaboration. I am deeply grateful to all of them and I wish to thank them very much for the part they played in creating this book.

I remember quite well the summer day in Oslo when I proposed the plan for my project to Ian Westbury. Not only did he encourage me, he helped me to find a publisher; he was a severe, though understanding critic in every detail; and he is introducing me to a public unknown to me. I thank Ian for that with all my heart! When I spoke of "our" book at one point he rejected this language. I think he was right only in the sense that I am responsible for any remaining mistakes in these pages.

Some of the chapters have been previously published. I thank the following publishers and editors for permission to present a revision of the original publication in this book.

Chapter 1 was originally presented at a "Didaktik meets Curriculum" symposium at the IPN, Kiel, Germany, in October 1993. This paper was published as "Some Remarks on Research in Education and Didactics in Germany" (in Hopmann & Riquarts, 1995). The chapter also appeared in German translation (in S. Hopmann & K. Riquarts [Eds.]. [1995]. *Didaktik und/oder Curriculum. Grundprobleme einer international vergleichenden Didaktik* [pp. 115–126]. Basel: Weinheim and Basel 33. *Beiheft der Zeitschrift für Pädagogik.*

Chapter 5 was originally presented at the AERA meeting at New Orleans, USA, in April 1994; a substantially revised version appears as "Content: Still in Question?" (in I. Westbury, S. Hopmann, & K. Riquarts [Eds.] [2000]. *Teaching as a reflective practice: The German didaktik tradition.* Mahwah, NJ: Lawrence Erlbaum Associates.

Chapter 6 was originally presented at a "Didaktik meets Curriculum" meeting at Aarau, Switzerland, in October 1991. This paper was published in 1995 as "Didactics As Construction of Content," in the *Journal of Curriculum Studies,* pp. 353–371. The paper also appeared in Spanish translation as "Didactica como construccion de contenido," in *Revista de Estudios del Curriculum* (1998), pp. 21–41.

Chapter 7 was orignially published as "Throwing Two Dice. The Content of a Math Lesson" in the *Journal of Curriculum Studies* (1987), pp. 219–225. The paper also appeared in Spanish translation as "Arrojar dos dados: el contenido de una lección de matemáticas" in *Revista de Estudios del Curriculum* (1998), pp. 175–185.

Chapter 8 was originally presented at the Didaktik meets Curriculum symposium at the University of Oslo, Norway, in August 1995, and at the Stockholm Institute of Education in February 1996. It was published as "The Formation of Conscience: A Lost Topic of Didaktik" (in B. B. Gundem & S. Hopmann [Eds.] [1998]. *Didaktik and/or curriculum. An international dialogue* [pp. 227–253].

American University Studies Series, XIV Education, Vol. 41. New York: Lang. A substantially revised German version was published as "Bildung des Gewissens— Kann man zur Toleranz erziehen?" (in B. Jank & J. Vogt [Eds.] [1998]. *Ästhetische Erfahrung und ästhetisches Lernen* [Dokumentation Erziehungswissenschaft. Schriften aus dem FB 06 der Universität Hamburg, Vol. 13]).

Chapter 9 was originally presented at the ISCHE XX conference at Kortrijk, Belgium, in August 1998. A German translation is to be published as "Bilder— Bildung—Weltbild," in *Paedagogica Historica*.

Peter Menck
Siegen, July 1999

Introduction

Ian Westbury

Several years ago, I shared with an American colleague a copy of a paper by Arnold Kirsch on "simplification" in mathematics teaching (Kirsch, 1976, 2000) that I had been given at a seminar in Berlin and had found to be quite fascinating as a form of curriculum research that I had never seen before. My colleague got back to me quickly agreeing that the paper was indeed both novel and very interesting, and went on to ask where the paper came from and what it represented. I told him that the paper had been described to me as an example of "classical" *Gymnasium* didactics. Predictably he asked what *Gymnasium* didactics was and I had to say that I did not know.

Some time later I was able to pose the question "What is didactics?" to colleagues in Europe. They told me that didactics, or (more properly) Didaktik, was the long-standing and highly elaborated heart of thinking about teaching in Germany; and that *Didaktik der Mathematik* of the kind Kirsch's paper represented was but one part of the much larger Didaktik tradition—and but one of many papers of a similar kind. As a result of these discussions, we were able to form a European-American seminar, which we called the "Didaktik meets Curriculum" group,[1] with the goal—on the part of the Americans in the group—of coming to terms with the Didaktik tradition. Peter Menck was a member of our group and as I read and discussed the papers he presented in our meetings, I became fascinated with them—both as an instantiation and a development of what Didaktik was and also, more importantly, for what they were: a sustained attempt to work through a set of fundamental and universal questions about schooling, albeit in what were for me at that time unusual ways.

As I came to understand as a result of the meetings of our group, these papers by Peter Menck were expressions of a *Bildung-centered Didaktik*, an application to teacher education of the German traditions of *Bildungstheorie* (theory of *Bildung*), and of the "human-science" educational theory, *geisteswissenschaftliche Pädagogik*, which had emerged in the early 20th century as an interpretation of the implications for education of the thought of the German philosopher, Wilhelm Dilthey (1833–1911). These highly elaborated traditions of educational theory and research, which are fundamental to teacher education in Germany, are largely unknown in the English-speaking world—a result of the separation of Anglo-American educational thinking from the German tradition that began in the years before the First World War, and that has continued, for political and cultural reasons, until today.[2] But, as this volume by Peter Menck makes clear, that wall between two cultures has been like an observation-room mirror: The English-speaking world knows little or nothing of either classical or contemporary work within the traditions of *Bildungstheorie*, *Pädagogik*, and Didaktik, but the German world has observed the Anglo-American world. Sometimes that world has been picked up and moved to Germany lock, stock, and barrel; at other times, it has been viewed selectively, and incorporated within the traditional German frame.

In this book, we see an example of this latter approach. Peter Menck explores here a set of fundamental problems in what we Americans would call curriculum theory, but his discussion is different from anything that has been written within curriculum theory in what he looks at, and how he uses what he sees. And while he draws heavily in some places on English-language educational research, the framing and substance of the arguments he develops are different from our patterns of argument, and totally embedded in the German tradition. It is this heritage that makes his questions, and his arguments, so unlike anything in English-language curriculum theory. But it is just this "German perspective" that also makes the essays in this book so rewarding to non-Germans: A new world of questions about classrooms, textbooks, and the history of schooling is opened up in compelling ways to enrich our understanding of the questions around English-language curriculum and pedagogical theorizing and research.

But, as Peter Menck also says in Chapter 2, it is difficult to transfer a German perspective, with its understandings and conceptions, into the English-language conceptual and linguistic framework. The language, culture, and ideologies, and the structures, traditions, and history of German education differ significantly from those of the English-language world. With these differences come different concepts and terms, connotations, and, ultimately, meanings.[3] It is important to acknowledge this "problem" at several levels as one approaches the chapters in this volume, and Menck explores some of these differences in perspective. However, let me underline those discussions by sketching *some* of the major themes in German educational thinking.[4] I will then offer my own reading of where Menck is coming from. I hope I can in this way complement his own discussions and, in doing so, make the case for the importance of his thinking, and the thinking of his tradition, for English-language curriculum theory and educational research.

As I have already indicated, this book is a work from within the traditions of *Bildungstheorie*, human-science education theory, and Didaktik. Thus Menck's starting point stems from the human-science (that is, *Geisteswissenschaft*), tradition of educational theory, which has in its turn close links with the German movement of "reform" (that is, progressive), pedagogy. In this tradition, educational theory and research are not seen as detached studies of the ideas or institutions of education, schooling, instruction, or learning, but rather as activities animated by a commitment on the part of both scholars and teachers to think actively and reflectively, and in complex, practice-based ways, about the cultural and societal work of schooling. Human-science educational theory—and theorizing—sought, and seeks, to understand education in ways that give priority to practice, are historically aware, and take into account the past, present, and future to emphasize the complexities embedded in the culture and society, and in schooling, teaching, and learning (see Gundem, 1998). The tradition seeks to offer a comprehensive basis for *engaged reflection* on educational practice by educators and teachers who have "the will to understand" their work, and its context. In the often-quoted words of Wilhelm Flitner which Menck invokes in Chapter 1, the "objects [of educational theory and research] are . . . children, adolescents in so far as they need educating, *Bildung*, vocational training. . . . They are seen as *homines educandi* [that is, people to be educated]." The test of educational theorizing with this end in view, and the perspective it offers, is whether or not teachers are enabled to think more reflectively about what they are doing. Thus, what we have in this book is as much the stuff of teacher education as it is educational research—and, indeed, the chapters of this book have their origins in the comprehensive introduction to education that Peter Menck has taught for many years to undergraduate teacher education students at the University of Siegen.

The second tradition at the center of this volume is Didaktik which, as I said earlier, is at heart of German thinking about teaching and provides the language of German teacher education and teaching. Didaktik is an umbrella concept that pulls into one frame a body of traditions that offer ways of thinking about the what, the how, and, most importantly, the why questions around teaching.[5] It is a body of traditions, both of research and of practices within teacher education, that differ from those found in the Anglo-Saxon world of "methods" and "curriculum and instruction" in its emphasis on teachers' *rationales* for actions and decisions within the classroom. And while there are many Didaktik language and dialects (and a *Fachdidaktik* for every subject area), for much of this century the dominant "progressive" forms in both theorizing and "practical" teacher education have been Bildung-centered, based on the two-centuries-old tradition of *Bildungstheorie*. To come to terms with this Didaktik, and with the chapters in this book, we have to unpack the concept of *Bildung*; Menck does this in Chapters 2 and 6 with more authority than I can, but let me selectively foreshadow his discussion.

Since its emergence as a distinct scholarly field in the late 19th century, all German educational theory and research, *Pädagogik*, has been grounded in the

Enlightenment idea and ideal of *Bildung*. This concept, which has a complex web of associations and connotations around it deriving from both its origins in religious thought and its subsequent appropriation by both the philosophers of the German Enlightenment and German educational and cultural ideologies, is commonly translated as "education," but it is better associated with the notion around the English word "formation" as found in such phrases as "character formation." Thus the word *Bildung* pulls into one concept-web the ideas of both the *forming* or shaping of the higher forces of the self, personality or—perhaps better—"soul" into a unity as well as the product of this forming, the particular *formedness* that is represented in the person (see Witz, 2000). In the theory of *Bildung* such forming, and the resulting formedness, is always an outcome of a person's *self-activity*, of an interaction between the cultural patterns in the human-made material, cultural, social, and moral worlds we inhabit and the subjective experience of those patterns. We appropriate the patterns of our world, which are when all is said and done the achievement and the products of humanity, so that "humanity" penetrates our social and cultural nature and we become formed individual expressions of the human achievements we have experienced. This process of forming, and the subsequent formedness, is inevitably a *self*-formation: The form of my formedness emerges as I come to terms and appropriate, in ways that penetrate my mind and heart, the worlds I inhabit and encounter.

As I have suggested, the idea of *Bildung* became part of the language around German schooling as a cipher for what might be thought of as the rationale for and the task of the educational system as one of the major formative institutions of the society. Teaching came to be seen as creating "classrooms"—physical settings, materials, and subject matters and social interactions—that reflect *Bildung*, the German cultural ideals, *and* evoke self-forming responses from students that respond to those cultural ideals.[6]

The human-science educational theory that emerged in Germany in the late 19th century sought to understand the relationship between the changing manifestations of *Bildung* seen in various cultures and periods and their forming institutions. *Bildung*-centered Didaktik undertook the task, which was central to teacher education, of understanding the ways in which formation is, can, and might be supported by the practices of the classroom (for example, by the cultural forms and societal practices that students experience through the various kinds of "work" we ask them to do). *Bildung*-centered Didaktik in this sense seeks to bring to the consciousness of teachers this interaction between the offers for formative self-activity that they make and the resulting subjective work by students that in turn lead to their self-formation. It seeks to give teachers and others involved in the work of the schools the capacity to understand and recognize what they do, and might do better, in creating forms of "instruction" that are both potentially *self-formative*, and reflect the habits of thought and sensibility we associate with a mature cultural *formedness*. For *Bildung*-centered Didaktik, the central term is *Allgemeinbildung*, an all-round, general rather than a subject-based formedness.

To put it more formally, *Bildung*-centered Didaktik is "a theory of educative [that is, formative] contents . . ., of their structure and selection, their teaching and learning objectives, and the teaching and learning tasks that can be assigned to them" (Künzli, 2000, p. 43) *and* "a theory of pedagogical action in relation to the question of the 'personal transfer of ideational contents from person to person'" (p. 46). In the words of Erich Weniger (1894–1961), one of the leading theorists of *Bildung*-centered Didaktik of the interwar and early postwar years:

> Didaktik subjects everything that happens in instruction to its observation. We call the structured context within which the growing generation is taught and knowledge is handed down the "order of teaching". . . . The order of teaching is thus the specific connection of factors and elements in which adolescents—or indeed anyone engaged in a learning, assimilating or developing process—interact with the world of values, with objective intellect, with society, with the adult generation, and where education takes place. . . . Order of teaching is the system which is imposed or simply used to achieve formative . . . encounters, or confrontation, with the intellectual, historical and social world . . . to achieve acceptance of the world by the younger generation. (Weniger, 2000, p. 112)

And, reflecting his grounding in *geisteswissenschaftliche Pädagogik*, Weniger goes on to emphasize that such a Didaktik cannot be universalizing in ideological, normative, institutional, or "practical" senses:

> With the historicity of its object, Didaktik itself becomes historical, i.e., it cannot present insights of universal and eternal validity, but must always strive to understand the changing situation, and from there *reshape the theory of action*. . . . (Weniger, 2000, p. 113, emphasis added)

Needless to say, the obvious question is, how do we approach this task of developing such a Didaktik, or an analogous "curriculum theory," with the capacity to shape and reshape theories of pedagogical action? This has been the central task for theorizing and for research within the *Bildung*-centered Didaktik tradition, and is it the task Menck has undertaken in the chapters in this volume, but in a way that is quite different from Weniger's.

We can see this difference, and thus understand more clearly what Menck is seeking to do in the chapters in this book, by comparing his starting point with the starting point Weniger invoked to structure his comprehensive and still relevant Didaktik built around an understanding of the curriculum. In Weniger's (2000) words:

> It may be argued that the order of teaching should be sought and portrayed at any point where teaching takes place. After all, as the whole is present in all of the component parts, it could be depicted through any one of the details. Thus it would seem appropriate to address oneself to the immediate pedagogical relationship and to gauge from this the whole, the structure of the order of teaching. (p. 114)

xvi LOOKING INTO CLASSROOMS

But, as he goes on to observe, ". . . this would be a most arduous task. . . . Therefore we must ask whether the order of teaching has already been represented, possibly conceptually, at some point, and is already accessible to us" (p. 114).

For Weniger, a representation of the order of teaching in institutionalized schooling was to be found in *Lehrpläne*, the state-mandated syllabuses that have long prescribed what was to be taught in German schools—but not the teaching methods, which were and are the exclusive responsibility of teachers. Thus his Didaktik was built around the codification of the "order of teaching" found in *Lehrpläne*, on the grounds that "all reflection in Didaktik can be linked to a theory of the *Lehrplan*" (p. 114). His *Bildung*-centered Didaktik became an exploration of the relationship between the subject matter contents set out in *Lehrpläne* and both the larger cultural order and the aspiration, which he saw as part and parcel of the teaching profession, to offer opportunities for formation to young people. His Didaktik was a *Lehrplantheorie*, or a curriculum theory.

Peter Menck, on the other hand, has accepted the challenge that Weniger recognized, but said would be arduous, and has sought to explore "the immediate pedagogical relationship and . . . [gauge] from this the whole, the structure of the order of teaching." In the chapters in this book, he seeks to show us how we can look in and at classrooms historically, empirically, and conceptually to discern the "order of teaching" that they reflect. His questions, which he asks again and again in the pages that follow, are:

- What image of human achievements, and the always human-made world, is being produced, and thus made available to pupils, by the work done in the classroom? What is the "pedagogical reality" that is, what is the reality of humankind, being presented in this classroom? Or in this classroom situation?
- How do teachers go about presenting their pupils, young people, with the offers that lead them to engage themselves with the culture, and thus become formed?
- What formative work do pupils do in response to the offers that teachers build into the work that *they* ask pupils to engage in?
- And, finally and fundamentally, how can we approach and think about these questions?

Thus, he asks of the contemporary classrooms he observes: What image of a culturally significant formedness—of what kind?—inheres, for example, in the content and the pedagogy of this math lesson?[7] What role might the school be playing in the formation of people who, for example, not only recognize right and wrong, but are *committed* to do right?[8] What determines the didactic or pedagogical logic of this or that move by the teacher in this art lesson—with its implications for the kind of classroom work he or she is asking pupils to engage in? How do Beate and Manuela understand *their* work in *this* art lesson? And what might this mean for our understanding of the pedagogical realities offered in this lesson?[9] And always, he embeds his understanding of contemporary classrooms with his observations of past classrooms, or at least the images that we can construct of those classrooms. As he weaves his questions and answers—about past and present classrooms—together, he builds a *Bildung*-centered picture of the class-room, of what it does and how it works, that is rich and realistic, and at many points a challenge to the reform-pedagogical heritage of the Didaktik tradition—and to the progressivism that is the heritage of the curriculum theory tradition.

Menck's analysis is deeply embedded in his perspective on schooling and his understanding of *Bildung*. Thus, he is in a sense sanguine about what teachers and schools do in creating environments that support formation, although he recognizes that what schools do is deeply penetrated by issues of power and class that need to be brought to consciousness—and that humankind does have a capacity for evil which forms of schooling have nurtured, and could again nurture. His question is not then normative in that he seeks a new or different understanding of what schools might or could be. We have, when all is said and done, such prescriptions in abundance! Instead, as Menck sees it, the overwhelming immediate task facing educational theory is the recognition and understanding of what schooling and classrooms have achieved, and are achieving, through their inherited practices and the day-to-day work of their teachers. It is this achievement of educational *practice* that must be understood—and educational theory and Didaktik must be realigned so that rather than being a search for (usually unrealizable) new, it can bring to reflective consciousness the work that schools actually do.

We can see the thrust of this point of view most clearly perhaps in Chapter 8, where Menck discusses the fundamental problem of the formation, that is, *Bildung*, of character and conscience, the relationship between knowledge and conscience, and the role of the school in the forming of dispositions to the good. Thus, for Menck any reflection on the role of schools in the formation of conscience must begin by recognizing that people *do* distinguish right from wrong and they *do* develop dispositions or habits that lead them to act on their understandings of right and wrong, the appropriate and the inappropriate. The question for educational theory is what part might or do schools play in this formation? And, as he goes to argue, while this question has been widely acknowledged as a central problem for both educational theory and Didaktik, we have not been able to articulate a plausible framing of the question, and certainly no persuasive answer. And, because we do not see how moral formation might be happening in the school, both educationists and the public assume that it does not happen, or that what is happening is somehow inappropriate. So, we are moved to make prescriptions about how to undertake what is missing—through character training or education, through values or affective education, through the posting of the Ten Commandments on school bulletin boards, and the like. Or, we construct "utopias" in response to perceived failures of the school or culture without specifying how these utopias might come into existence or, more importantly, might be connected with what schools already do.

But, as Menck goes on to ask, can we reasonably assume that a major socializing institution, and an institution that has been at the center of the culture for time out of mind, has failed to come to terms with the central formative issues of moral or character formation? With the formation of dispositions to the good, to tolerance, humaneness, decency, and so on? Can we reasonably assume that the school has failed to construct pedagogical realities in which moral questions are central and in which children and adolescents are led to come to terms with humanity's central moral understandings?

As he considers these problems, Menck asks us to look for a "hidden curriculum" which he sees as the heart of the formative offer that shows to pupils the interpenetration of the understanding of the good, which the schools address in their formal curriculum, and the disposition to the good. This hidden curriculum is represented in the symbolic worlds being represented and created by the illustrations and stories in classical and contemporary textbooks. This world of "pictures and stories," and the discursive contexts that teachers create around them, invite interpretation, reflection, and discussion—knowledge—of the situations they depict. And, by virtue of the "aesthetic" and emotional power of pictures and stories, there is also the potential in these stories and pictures for engaging commitment to the world they order and represent; they are *offers* to pupils of a moral reality, albeit in symbolic form, which has the potential to form the conscience and well as the mind.

And, as Menck shows in Chapter 9, these same processes take place on the larger canvas of a *Weltbild*, an image of the world that encapsulates both *usus atque abusus*, use and abuse, *scientia* and *conscientia*, knowledge and conscience, and people's understanding of first and last things. Thus, the pictures, and the situations embedded in them, and the stories told around them, both represent and offer an image of a *Weltbild*, a world-view, "in a symbolic way" *and* are presented in pedagogical contexts in such a way that "pupils are able to recognize themselves in the stories and in the pictures." They can, Menck suggests, place themselves in the world that is pictured in these stories and illustrations, and, as they do this, they find themselves introduced into the moral order "without force," because the pedagogical, didactic situation in which they are presented and interpreted demands acceptance of the "validity for the underlying order and the behavioral norms embedded in [that] order" (p. 122). It is the ordinariness of this environment that hides it from the view of the theorist and leads to the conviction that something important is missing from the curriculum—when it is in fact everywhere, everyday!

In Chapters 8 and 9, and indeed throughout this book, Menck invokes, and discusses extensively, the classical textbooks and primers of Comenius and Basedow, as his icons of both the potentially formative symbolic moral order and of the pedagogical logics that are found in every classroom. But, in proceeding in this way, he wants us to learn from the history of education in some particular ways. Thus, as he writes in the last paragraphs of Chapter 9:

At a time when the "loss of an objective order" . . . is earnestly discussed, when the lack of a binding orientation seems to give every reason for worry by educationalists, and when, with a postmodern attitude, things are left to individual discretion, it may be helpful to remember the topic of the identity of *scientia* and *conscientia*. There have been times when knowledge of the world was supposed, with a nearly logical necessity, to imply motives to act rightly. . . .

Our two classical educationalists were not the only ones we could have called on: My two examples are simply special cases. . . . And today, we find books like [Comenius's] *Orbis Sensualium Pictus*, or at least like some of its chapters, in our schools as primers and reading books. It would be a rewarding task to analyze all those many editions, or rather revised versions, that have derived from the *Orbis Pictus*. In all of the books that either directly reinterpret the *Orbis Pictus* or draw knowingly or unknowingly on its inspiration, the pictures that are drawn and the stories that are told teach the children how the world and things in the world correlate. They convey a judgment about what is true and what is false and *at the same time* they convey an opinion about good and evil—whether they intend to do so or whether it happens by itself. (p. 123)

In other words, he invites us as teachers to ask *his* questions of *our* world, and in so doing he makes an offer for our formation that, if accepted, can lead us to shape—or reshape—our theory of action.

We see this form of argument in every chapter in this book. Menck looks at the history of schooling as one in which we have learned to create settings, an "order of teaching," that refract or mirror symbolically what is most essential in our cultures. He also asks us to recognize that these symbols are, moreover, instantiated in pedagogical practices that invite and encourage pupils to engage with them, to interpret them for themselves. This two-sided hidden curriculum, of symbols and practices, is *not* one that serves to counter in some covert way the ideal curriculum. It *is* the curriculum that forms; that is, it is the educative, the formative, environment of the school. But it can only be seen as educative, as forming, if we approach it with a conception of the idea of formedness, the *Bildung*, that it is inevitably instantiating.

In the chapters of this book, Menck shows us how this hidden curriculum of *Bildung* can be surfaced and become the object of attention, and interpreted for what it tells us about the culture that is being offered to our students. As he does this, Menck at times subjects fragments from classrooms that he has observed or others have described to his interpretative lens; more often he looks at the history of schooling, to the work of Comenius, Luther, and others that we English-speakers know less well. He traces a path from a *Weltbild*, from a cultural practice, such as mathematics or the school orchestra, or from a reflection of a societal practice, such as battery poultry farming, to the pedagogy of the offer we make to students. This book is a search for an understanding of how this or that symbolic instantiation of human reality that is classroom work might form, to use his words, the "little ones"—and those who are not so little—as they grapple with what they have been invited to experience.

But, Menck's starting point is always practice. He asks in each of his instances what it is that is being expressed, and what it is that we value, in terms of *Bildung*—culture—in this or that instance, and how this or that instance can be seen as formative and as reflecting and contributing to human formedness, both good and bad. And he notes that in this search for understanding, "The common (and commonly) 'bad' practice *and* 'progressive' innovations are all significant . . ." (p. 52, emphasis in original). In writing in this way, he opens up the classroom that we have inherited for interpretation as an aspect of the human achievement. In so doing, he is also asking us to engage with particular achievement, the classroom, and open our world-views as teachers, to learn something about ourselves. In other words, this book, and each of its chapters, is an offer to teachers that is itself framed in the terms of *Bildungstheorie* and Didaktik in that it seeks through stories, pictures, and analysis to engage *us* in interpretation of a set of symbols of the classroom, and thus in a self-formative process. It invites us to reflect and rereflect on practice, and in the manner of *Bildung*-centered teaching, to think about our theories of classroom action.

1

Research In Education and Didactics in Germany

Let me, as I begin, adopt the point of view of an ethnomethodologist. When the proverbial person from Mars, or an educationalist from abroad, tries to follow German discourse on education and on classrooms in school, he or she might be reminded of Shakespeare's Hamlet (Act II, scene II):

"What do you read, my lord?"
"Words, words, words."
"Slanders, sir . . ." (Follows a heap of nonsense—Polonius aside:)
"Though this be madness, yet there is method in't."

What Hamlet is reading does not make sense to Polonius; the picture is too confusing. He assumes, however, that it has some kind of meaning, and, as we know, it really has. What is the meaning that underlies that German didactical discourse?

In the German history of research in education, two approaches to research on classrooms and teaching can be identified.

■   The older of the two traditions dates back to the first of the so-called "didacticians," Wolfgang Ratke (1571–1635) with his *Die neue Lehrart* (The New

1

Way of Teaching) and Johann Amos Comenius (1592–1670) with his famous *Didactica magna* (The Great Didactic), and proceeds to the textbooks on Didaktik of our day. It may be characterized as follows: Teachers gain experience while preparing, giving, and evaluating lessons. These experiences are collected and organized as a knowledge of teaching, which aims at serving as a medium of professional studies. This knowledge is enriched, updated, and evaluated by each generation of teachers and educationists.

- The other approach begins with Ernst Christian Trapp (1745–1818), who, in his *Versuch einer Pädagogik* (Essay on Education), was the first to ask for the gathering of data on the classroom and its environment. Some 100 years later, the teachers' associations organized empirical research in education. Their work was later continued by psychologists and educationalists, and has been enhanced since the late 1950s by the acceptance of Anglo-American understanding of both educational research and the issues it should and could address. This tradition now has a distinguished body of both researchers and readers of journals such as the *Unterrichtswissenschaft* (Classroom Research) and compendia like the *Handbuch für Curriculumforschung* (Handbook of Curriculum Studies).

Both of these approaches aim to understand what happens in education, and particularly in classrooms. Both have their shortcomings, so that one could say, and actually it has been said, that they do not fully achieve their respective purpose. The German educationalist Peter Petersen (1884–1952) tried to bring those traditions together in the 1920s and 1930s, and I will draw on his idea of a pedagogically oriented research in education and outline my way toward a theory of didactics.

"PEDAGOGICAL RESPONSIBILITY"—A CLUE TO GERMAN DIDAKTIK

The concept of "pedagogical responsibility" seems to be the key to understanding and addressing the problems within the contemporary didactical discourse in Germany. In order to explain this concept, let me invoke Wilhelm Flitner's (1958) formula: "Educational science is *reflexion engagée*" (engaged reflection).

> Educational science is reflection from the point of view of a responsible educator. Its objects are . . . children, adolescents in so far as they need educating, *Bildung,* vocational training. . . . They are seen as *homines educandi*. (p. 18, my translation)[10]

Flitner's concept was applied to Didaktik by Wolfgang Klafki (1963), who based his definition of "the didactical field" on the:

. . .pedagogical responsibility towards young people, who are obliged to fulfil the sense of their lives as children and adolescents and, at the same time, to grow step by step towards their autonomy. Here, in pedagogical responsibility, we have the "general authority" for didactical decisions, and here we have the link to all other areas of educational acting and thinking. The center of this responsibility is the child or youth who needs help in order to gain his or her autonomy and personal responsibility, and who shall be enabled to manage all situations of [his or her life] in a human way, whether it is in the present or in the future. (p. 101)[11]

I believe that this concept of "pedagogical responsibility" gives an essential clue to the understanding of the German Didaktik. Above all, this concept offers some ways of avoiding some crucial restrictions from which our present didactical discourse seems to suffer. But, before speaking of restrictions, let us step on a relatively firm ground, namely the practice of *Unterricht* (classroom).

DIDACTICS—AN EXPLANATION AND TWO TYPES

Unterricht is something like an anthropological datum. When we observe human beings in society, wherever or whenever they live, we find a practice that consists of *passing on* (the Latin "traditio") *of knowledge,* either relatively informally or formally institutionalized in classrooms of modern schools. The indispensable requisites of that practice are:

- One who *administers* knowledge (a "traditor"): a priest, a catechist, a teacher, in any case a representative of the elder generation
- *Innocent youth*
- *Knowledge,* administered by the one and necessary for the present and future lives of the others

The rest is optional, as, for example, the classrooms and formal organizations such as the school in which the practice of *Unterricht* is embedded in our societies.[12] It is this practice in modern classrooms in a modern school—in short, the "classroom"—that we German educationists talk about. Insofar as we refer to this practice when communicating and researching, we understand one another and are able to look for the adequate terms.

Now I want to introduce another term, namely *didactics*, although I am afraid that my usage might have a pejorative connotation in English.[13] But just as "physics" comprises all knowledge of inanimate nature, we should look for a notion that captures all the knowledge that has to do with classroom, and everything happening inside it. So I would like to suggest "didactics." Thus, we have:

- Didactical models: models of the classroom

- Didactical theory: theory of the classroom in its context
- Didactical research: classroom research
- Didactical technique: the art of managing the classroom, and so on

I must stress that the notion of "didactics" is not restricted to teaching; it refers to classroom as a whole.[14] In this way I adopt a point of view that is outside the classroom: from the outside I am trying to get an insight into what happens *inside* the classroom.

Looking at the writing about the classroom from this outside point of view, we soon become aware of two main ways of looking at classrooms found in the German Didaktik. Indeed, one can even speak of two camps of didacticians who have their own slogans, methods, topics, and intentions and, as seen in their representatives, do not overlap. One of the camps is crowded with those who call themselves "didacticians." Again and again they explicate what the classroom should be like and how, accordingly, instruction has to be carried out. The knowledge they administer and produce ranges widely—from philosophical discussions of basic terms such as *Bildung* or *Methode* to cookbooks for the preparation of teacher-proof lessons. This knowledge is the product of teachers' experiences—at best the experiences of generations, or at worst the authors' idiosyncrasies. Of late, this has been offered in the form of so-called "didactical models"; these models were meant to be, and have actually been, simple and useful manuals used in training teachers before they were philosophically converted into "paradigms."

In the other camp are the "empiricists." Empirical research on teaching and learning, *Lehr–Lern–Forschung*, is their slogan; the *Zeitschrift für empirische Pädagogik* (Journal for Research on Education) and *Unterrichtswissenschaft*—with the emphasis, on "*-wissenschaft*" (research)—are their media of communication; and the *Arbeitsgemeinschaft für Empirische Pädagogische Forschung* (Association for Empirical Pedagogical Research), their organization. This work, and the knowledge it has produced, is the equivalent of the empirical pedagogical research of both the English-speaking world and Scandinavia.

I am not saying that these camps debate each other; the one does simply not take much notice of the other.[15] This is surprising as both seek to produce and administer knowledge about classroom. It is also a pity because there are many indications that neither camp really achieves what it is aiming at, *the improvement of the practice of instruction at school.*

ROOTS—THE "METHOD IN IT"

I have not highlighted these two extreme positions to criticize one-sided points of view in the German didactical discourse. That would neither be very original, nor would it be historical because as we look into the history of German Didaktik we can see that there were very reasonable motives that led to the development of both of these traditions.

The "Didacticians"

Again and again we Germans are reminded, with good reason, of the fact that the term "didactics" or "Didaktik" has been used since the time of the so-called "didacticians"—Ratke and Comenius in particular. Originally the Latin word "didactica" was used as if it were an adjective to which the noun "ars" (art) had to be added; Ratke precisely translated "ars didactica" into *Lehrkunst* (the art of teaching). And in Comenius's famous *Didactica Magna* (Great Didactic) we find the pattern that was to be the basis for all didactical reasoning to come:

- First, there are some tenets, and beliefs about the destination of human beings, about their "nature," as Comenius puts it.
- Then, a criticism of the school, which—as he saw it—prevented young people from attaining their goals.
- This was combined with the concept of a better school.
- Finally, rules were devised according to which children should be taught in this better school; rules derived from age-old experience and legitimized for him by the Holy Bible, by "the old" (that is, philosophers), by nature (here, above all, by the way birds live), and by the rules of human craft and technology.[16]

The reasonable idea in this tradition is, as I see it, that the classroom has always been interpreted *as posing practical tasks*. This theory of the "didacticians" finds its bearings in the practice of successful teaching.

The "Empiricists"

If the classroom is interpreted as posing tasks, the implication is, historically, the professionalization of teaching. Chairs of education were established in all European countries (compare Hopmann & Riquarts, 1995) and, when we Germans reflect on this, we never forget to refer to Ernst Christian Trapp.[17] Trapp, like Comenius, not only compiled rules for education, but he went further: He aimed at a complete system of education, a well-founded and complete set of rules to make sure that "children are helped to gain autonomy" (Trapp, 1977, p. 59, my translation).

> If we had a fitting number of correctly made pedagogical observations and reliable experiences we could write down a correct and complete system of pedagogics. . . . And if we had this system we could put public education and teaching into a state in which nothing is left to be altered or improved. (pp. 61–62).

This is, of course, an outline for an empirical educational science. Such a science began to take shape 100 years or so later when the teachers' associations began to support and carry out empirical educational research.

In a subtle study, the Belgian educationist Marc Depaepe (1993) reconstructed this process step by step. He presented a very detailed survey of what today is called empirical educational research and organized the research around the paradigms of child-study, "pedology,"[18] experimental educational science, and educational psychology. What Depaepe reconstructed was a movement that can be characterized by specific questions about education derived from practical problems in the classroom and by the attempt to develop specific research methods.

In Germany, the large variety of experimental educational research faded away in the late 1920s. According to Depaepe, this process was a result of the predominance of human-science pedagogy in the 1920s, of the increasing orientation toward psychology, and then word of the deformation during the Third Reich.

Today there is at best reference to the work of two outstanding representatives of that "empiric" movement in German Didaktik, Wilhelm Lay (1862–1926) and Ernst Meumann (1862–1915), who are at least known by the title of their main works, *Experimentelle Didaktik* (Experimental Didactics; Lay, 1903) and *Abriss der experimentellen Pädagogik* (Outlines of Experimental Pedagogics; Meumann, 1914). They are seen as the founders of an empirical pedagogy, but usually only with the intention to illustrate contradictions. The empirical classroom research done in Germany today is based on assumptions and models that were imported from the United States in the late 1960s.[19]

A MISSING LINK?—"PEDAGOGICAL EMPIRICAL RESEARCH"

On the one hand, individual and passed-on experiences, which are generally not reflected upon, enter Didaktik as its empirical foundation. On the other hand, reliable knowledge is produced but it is often not evident how to use it. Taken together, one could say that didactical reasoning is, on the one hand, empirically blind, at least in one eye and, on the other hand, often insignificant in its practical consequences. At the beginning of this chapter, I suggested that shortcomings such as these could be avoided if the " human science concept" of Didaktik were taken as the theoretical basis. I come back to this suggestion now.

Let us return to history once more and look at Friedrich Schleiermacher's (1768–1834) *Lectures on Education* from 1826 (Schleiermacher, 1966).[20] He begins with the simple questions: Who needs a theory of education, and what is its subject? It is not a technique for the use of teachers. "It rather is a theory which is built upon the *relation between the older and the younger generation* and upon the obligations of the former towards the latter" (p. 9). In other words, the practice of education *as a whole* defines the object of educational theory. And, as Schleiermacher explicates in the course of his argument, this "whole" includes the child and its nature, educators, a pedagogical situation, institutions, and formal organizations. I believe it would now be useful to transfer Schleiermacher's definition to didactics: The object of didactical theory is the obligation to pass on the relevant culture. *This is what happens in the classroom and defines, in the strict sense of the word, the object of didactics*, or, *didactics is the theory of classroom practice.*

Erich Weniger (1894–1961), the academic mentor of most of the German didacticians who dominated the didactical discourse in the 1960s and 1970s,[21] defined "didactics" in this way and added an explanation:

> The classroom is more than simply the interaction of teaching and learning. . . . The classroom is the concrete context of factors in which youths . . . and the world of cultural assets, of society, of the older generation come together, one factor of this context being the will to organize classroom teaching. (Weniger, 1952, p. 5, my translation)

Weniger's "will" is equivalent to the "pedagogical responsibility" of Flitner that I sketched at the beginning of this chapter.

With this definition of didactics as the theory of classroom, all of us may be happy.[22] On the basis of this understanding there should be a way to unite both groupings of didacticians I distinguished earlier as well as different methods in order to aim at what I would call *an empirically founded didactics*. And we do not have to invent such a didactics: An empirically based didactics—the missing link, so to speak—exists.

We do not find such an empirically founded didactics behind the labels decorating the latest pedagogical fashions: open classrooms, humane school, free work, action-oriented, hands-on, or pupil-oriented didactics. Nevertheless, the idea of an empirically founded didactics has a venerable tradition. Let me return to Trapp again. He sought to arrange the body of age-old didactical rules systematically and to substantiate these rules empirically. He and his contemporaries, the philanthropists of the late 18th century, made these efforts in the *context* of a fundamental *reform of public schooling*. I say "in the context of" because classroom observation as such, and even a corpus of systematically arranged didactical rules, does not constitute reform in and of itself.

This possibility of linking both of these traditions—the empirical and the didactical one—becomes even more apparent when we look at the work of Werner Lay, Ernst Meumann, and their contemporaries. They studied empirically practical questions and problems of the classroom—arithmetic, orthography, attention, exercising. It was pedagogically or, rather, *didactically* and practically *defined topics* that determined their questions and their guiding terms. It was the classroom as a *paedagogicum*, as a pedagogical problem, in which our classical educationists— being teachers—were involved, and which they—being philosophers of education as well—tried to comprehend under the category of the "need" of education.

Werner Lay was the director of a teacher-training college; Ernst Meumann's first essay on experimental pedagogics was published in *Die Deutsche Schule* (The German School), the organ of the *Deutscher Lehrerverein* (German Teachers' Association). The latter dedicated his *Vorlesungen zur Einführung in die Experimentelle Pädagogik und ihre Psychologischen Grundlagen* (Introduction into Experimental Pedagogics and Its Psychological Elements) to the Königsberg, the Frankfurt and the Bremen Teachers' Association. I refer to this context in order to illustrate the practical involvement of their educational research. For Meumann, experimental pedagogy was a movement *"parallel to our contemporary effort of reforming public schooling"* (from Depaepe, 1993, p. 233, my emphasis). Its practical value lay "in the fact that the studies make teachers think about the ways and means they are using." That way, experimental pedagogics "increases the autonomy of the educator towards the pedagogical norm . . . and, at the same time, it gives him a greater interest in his work." (Depaepe, 1993, p. 223).

Peter Petersen had been one of Meumann's collaborators in the Hamburg Institute for Pedology, and for a short time his successor. In the 1930s, Petersen developed the concept of *pädagogische Tatsachenforschung* (empirical research in education), which was, and is, a genuinely *pedagogical* concept. This concept was linked with his well-known school at the University of Jena, the "Jena-Plan-School," in which he tried to bring together the best of the *Reformpädagogik* around the concepts of "group," "work," "life at school", "autonomy," and so forth. The realization of this model was accompanied by empirical research, the design of which Petersen developed and improved step by step, parallel to the development and dissemination of his school-model.

What did that *specifically pedagogical* research work look like? First of all, we have what Petersen called the "pedagogical situation."

> A pedagogical situation is an intentionally designed and supported setting, destined to provide the best help for the development, formation [*Bildung*], and maturing of the human potentials and the spirit of children and youths. It provides stimuli and manifold tasks for the youths, which is why everyone is obliged to react as a whole personality and to answer with relatively valid comments and performances. (Petersen, 1965, p. 109)

With this, I come back to my starting point, the concept of *pedagogical responsibility*. The objects of Petersen's pedagogical research are "pedagogical facts"— that is, factors or aspects of the "pedagogical situation": "Pedagogical facts are found in the behavior, the activity and the achievements of children and youths as well as of teachers and educators." The pedagogical characteristics of these facts are":

> (1) they reveal the development, formation (*Bildung*), and maturation of the human beings in relation to their . . . human nature. And (2) they are placed within an organization of the world of children or youths which is destined to support and to fur-

ther that development, *Bildung*, and maturing according to the idea of education. (p. 108)

It was Petersen's second wife, Else Müller-Petersen, who developed the method of pedagogical research along these lines as well as undertaking a significant body of research in Jena. Let us pick out just an example by chance in order to illustrate the idea behind it.

As one may easily see in Table 1.1, the entries reflect *group instruction* as an educational idea. Petersen's findings can be adequately interpreted only in the context of the *classroom as a "pedagogical situation."* They show Petersen's interest in a specific reform of *Unterricht* (classroom); his concern for supporting the assistance that pupils give each other while they are working—in contrast to following the teacher's orders. The empirical research served to establish whether the measures that were supposed to be taken here—group work and the development of a positive social climate—were as successful as he had hoped they would be.

Unfortunately the tradition reflected in Petersen and Müller-Petersen's research was interrupted after the Second World War. Some papers by Petersen and Müller-Petersen were published in the late 1940s, but the research work itself disappeared after the university school in Jena was closed in 1950. The more recent West German tradition of empirical classroom research that I described earlier dates from the importation from the English-speaking world of Kurt Lewin's studies of social climates and Ned A. Flanders's investigation of teaching styles (see Amidon & Hough, 1967).

CONCLUSION

The beginning of the 1990s saw several reviews of the empirical research undertaken since the 1960s. Summarizing these reviews, Uwe Hameyer (1990) stated

TABLE 1.1.   Distribution of Teachers' and Students' Assistance

Type of Assistance	Teacher Assists	Student Assists
Assistance in instruction	200	605
Work impulse	208	250
Assistance concerning the media	38	311
Assistance concerning school life	43	178
Order in the groups	11	48
Personal kindness	12	17
Total	512	1410

Source: Petersen, 1965, p. 409

that there is a "considerable range" of empirically proven knowledge about classrooms. However, he criticizes the lack of any "synthesis of today's knowledge about the processes of teaching and learning." The implication of detailed educational knowledge for the classroom practice is, according to him, only revealed "in connection with a comprehensive pedagogical perspective and critical reflection" (p. 24). Therefore, he feels the "need to coordinate knowledge with regard to a practical pedagogical objective" and "to evaluate knowledge according to pedagogical aims" (p. 25). His argument does not include any reference to Petersen's work, but reflects the traditions that I have called the "missing link" between the two contrary positions in German Didaktik. His argument is a plea for pedagogical empirical research—one century after the first attempts in the context of *Reformpädagogik* and half a century after the closure of Petersen's Jena-Plan-School in 1950.

What Hameyer asks for is a synthesis of knowledge that reconstructs lost contexts and combines fragments to a meaningful entirety. However, in view of the actual didactical discourse in Germany, it seems to be difficult to establish a common basis among us for such work. On the one hand, there are countless approaches to a "theory" of *lesson planning*—which is a practice of its own and which follows its own logic, let us say the logic of work-economy and work-effectiveness. On the other hand, there are *theories of psychological and social processes in classroom*; but while they are—admittedly—aspects of the classroom, these processes are certainly not *pedagogical* aspects. My discussion here of Petersen's concept of empirical classroom research is intended to underline the reality that there *is* an idea of an *empirically grounded didactics* in the German Didaktik tradition that aims at the investigation of the conditions for a successful practice of teaching *as well as* the structure and laws of teaching and learning. This is the idea that underlies the thinking and research I will be discussing in the remaining chapters of this book.

2

Bildung: A Core Concept of German *Didaktik*

Many educationalists from outside the German tradition of education know that *Bildung* is something like a core concept in German Didaktik. Yet when they read or hear this word, many feel uneasy about both the word and the concept—in the way we Germans do when we view the Black Forest, another typical German institution; we admire its beauty from afar, but we feel lost in the depths of the forest with its mountains, and its valleys. *Eine gebildete Person* (an educated person) is something nice to look at, but when German educationalists begin to explain what characterizes an "educated personality," they themselves have difficulties in understanding each other. Books and papers in which we try to explain what *Bildung* "really means" would fill a small library. I do not want to try to explore yet again what *Bildung* really means here. Instead, I will develop an operational definition of the concept of *Bildung* as a basis for my discussion on what happens in the classroom. In the second part of the chapter, I will ask what the modern school contributes to the process of an individual's *Bildung*. Or, from another point of view, in what way does *Bildung* serve as a criterion of didactical reasoning?

THE CONCEPT OF *BILDUNG*

So, what is *Bildung*? I will try to explain this word in the way that I understand it, and I will overlook the more subtle treatises produced by those of my colleagues who have closer links with philosophy.

Let me put it this way: When a person is born, he or she is *totally human* or is created in God's image, as the Christian tradition states it. But it is evident that this being is not only unable to walk, but also unable to read, write, count—and to tell lies. This child is also unaware that it could commit murder. In the course of the next few years, the child must first *acquire the attributes* that make him or her *human*. In all cultures there are institutions that regulate this stage of human life. And all cultures have initiation rites to conclude the stage when the characteristics stipulated by each culture as the minimum requirement have developed. Of course, the process does not finish there; it is left to the individual who may pursue it, or leave it at will.

Let us now imagine that our little green people managed to capture a specimen of the human race and take it back to Mars. If this specimen was to give its captors a relatively accurate picture of what "humans" really are, what should it be? Wilhelm von Humboldt (1767–1835), who left us a famous fragment on *Bildung* (written around 1790) and who was one of the founders of the modern *Gymnasium,* or academic secondary school, would say something along these lines: The specimen would have to be such "that the notion of humanity, should this be our one and only example, would acquire a greatness and dignity of content" (Humboldt, 1960, p. 236, my translation).

How does a human being achieve a status that represents, as perfectly as possible, what makes humans human? Humboldt answers simply, though somewhat obliquely, ". . . by combining our individual selves with the world in a process of most general, animated and free interaction" (Humboldt, 1960, pp. 235–236, my translation). Later, he adds what in my view is one of the central tenets of the Didaktik tradition, which is based on a theory of *Bildung*:

> What a human individual really needs is simply one object which makes interaction possible between receptivity and self-activity. If this object is to succeed in occupying its whole being in its entire strength and unity, then *this object must be the world itself . . . or at least considered as such.* (pp. 237–238, my translation, emphasis added)

It is Humboldt's phrase "considered as such" that opens up a field for fruitful didactical reasoning and practice.

Half a century later (1844), Karl Marx saw the world, objective reality, as the objectification of humankind's own self, with the implication that humankind itself becomes the object (see Marx, 1953, p. 241). How is this to be understood? Marx interpreted the "objects" in the "objective world" as objectifications of what the human being really is: these objectifications are documents from which we may learn what precisely a human being is. To this point, Marx's argument is a form of cultural anthropology, but the next step leads to the theory of *Bildung*. He maintained that it is only through these objectifications (for example, a painting by Picasso, a song by the Beetles, or the form of the Black Forest as it has been preserved over the generations), that the senses of a human being may be formed into *human* senses that can evaluate *beauty*. The—biological—eye and ear are transformed into the—human—senses of beauty of form. In other words, it is only in dealing with the objectifications—we could also say "culture"—that the human senses are engendered and cultivated. And this is not only true of the five senses, but also of the so-called intellectual and practical senses (will, love, and so on). The senses become human senses only through the existence of their object, through nature seen as the objectification of humankind, as Marx put it (see Marx, 1953, p. 242).

In this sense, discussing an area with which we associate him more readily, Marx describes the history of industry and the objectified existence of industry as the "human psychology" submitted to our senses; the "great industry" before our eyes documents the faculties of humankind and human beings: "In ordinary, material industry . . . we have before us in the form of sensuous, foreign, utilitarian objects . . . the objectified human faculties " (pp. 243–244, my translation).

What I reconstructed in the last paragraphs is what we Germans think of when we speak of *allgemeine* (general) *Bildung*. Within the framework of this philosophical tradition of discussion of *Bildung*, we can develop the following definition: *Bildung is the process in the course of which specific human beings acquire the characteristic human features.* This concept serves Didaktik as its theoretical bedrock for understanding what happens in the classroom. But these insights which have emerged from this distinctive tradition also provide a basis for a didactics, for a way of viewing the classroom that can extend far beyond the particular understandings of the German philosophical tradition.[23]

BILDUNG AND DIFFERENT AREAS OF DIDACTICAL REASONING

Now let me ask, what is the contribution of the modern school to the process of an individual's *Bildung*? Before I attempt to answer this question, let me introduce a distinction that may be helpful. It does not help to speak about "Didaktik" or "curriculum" in general; instead, we should distinguish between *different areas of didactical discourse*.[24] The problem of the theoretical foundation of didactics could then be discussed from, say, four different points of view:

■   From a *political* point of view: We can ask, which elements of a society's culture must, as a political necessity, be represented by the canon of school disciplines in both elementary and secondary schools?

- From the point of view of the *disciplines:* We can ask, what is the specific contribution of an academic discipline to the development toward humanity of a students' personality? This is the crucial question of a subject-matter didactics.
- From a *topic*-centered perspective: We can ask, in what way can we make a topic—whatever it might be—contribute to a person's *Bildung?*
- From the *classroom* perspective: We can ask, how should all of this be organized so that these persons, "my" students, see the abilities and knowledge they acquire during their work in the classroom as a contribution to their *Bildung?*

In Table 2.1, I present an overview of the areas of didactical discourse. I will now consider each of the issues I have identified here in more detail.

1. A culture must be passed on from one generation to another—unless we want to start from scratch again and again. By culture, I mean humanity's achievements in broadening its natural state of being so as to make possible a humane life in the world. *Bildung* as a criterion for didactical reasoning comes in as follows: Within this global and timeless process of the transmission of cultural tradition within a particular society, it is the task of the "school" to pass on a particular "cultural minimum," which will endow the young members of the particular culture with the achievements of humanity, thus turning them into full members of society. When this point has been reached, they have all the rights of an adult human being, they accept all the duties of an adult human being, and they have the abilities and the knowledge that allow them to make responsible use of their rights and to perform their duties.

The *curriculum of a school* which provides a *general* education—the elementary as well as secondary school—outlines the contents that are part of a society's cultural minimum: from the *enkyklios paideia* of the Greeks to the classical three R's and some more R's—such as religion, Art, and History of traditional European societies—and to the curriculum of a modern comprehensive school. The

TABLE 2.1.   **Areas of Didactical Discourse**

Point of View	Area of Didactical Discourse	Object to be Formed (gebildet)	Medium of *Bildung*
Political	Framing of the educational system	Human being	Culture
Disciplinary	Production of curricula	Dimensions of a personality	Mathematics
Topic-centered	Lesson planning textbook production	Specific abilities	Probability
classroom-centered	Organization of classroom work	Specific manifestation of an ability	David's and Ian's line

formation of the curriculum is a political process in which different interest groups with differing political power are involved. The concept of *Bildung* serves, as Erich Weniger (1999) put it, as a *pedagogical* criterion in the struggle for the curriculum.

2. The ancient Greeks standardized culture as a system of *disciplines*, an understanding that has not changed throughout the centuries. These disciplines describe, to put it in simplified terms, the bodies of knowledge defined by the different fields of practice of a society—systems of work or thought. The issues here are questions for subject matter didactics, or, as we say in German, of a *Fachdidaktik*.

The question of subject matter didactics is the "structure of the discipline." There are several bodies of knowledge competing with, or complementing, one another: mathematics here and everyday sums there; the beginner's arithmetic book on the one hand and Bourbaki on the other; or Euclid, Isaac Newton, or David Hilbert. Mathematical knowledge is used and produced in everyday life as well as in science; it can be presented as a system as well as in its development. At the same time the specific pedagogical criterion, *Bildung*, must be central to didactical discussion, and that implies the question, how can knowledge be organized so that dealing with it in school imparts specific abilities for coping with the specific challenges in everyday life? Since the days of Archimedes, for example, no one in the western world has doubted that mathematics is one of the most important achievements of the culture in its attempt to expand the seemingly fixed boundaries that lie in its nature. Since the *enkyklios paideia* of the Hellenistic Greeks, we rightly find *arithmetica* and *geometria* in the curriculum of compulsory schools, that is to say, schools that provide an *allgemeine Bildung* (general education). But this is not simply a matter of course. Whatever the argument may be from the point of view of mathematics as a science, the criterion of *Bildung* has to be applied to the math *curriculum*. The question is if, and to what extent, the ignorant or superstitious mind turns into a reasonably calculating one—just as the prehensile organ of the *Homo sapiens sapiens* is formed into a comforting and healing hand. This is what math, as well as physical education, seeks to achieve from the point of view of Bildung. The specimen of the species *Homo sapiens sapiens* must turn into a *Homo eruditus*.

3. Curricula specify *topics for classroom work*. By incorporating a topic into the curriculum, the responsible representatives of the adult generation express what is considered to be relevant for the education of the young. The German term for such a topic is *Bildungsinhalt*, "content of education." Of course, there is a process of transformation as a topic moves from the corpus of science to the curriculum; but the presence of a topic in the curriculum shows that it is thought to be something that will make an indispensable contribution to the education of the young.

But, this contribution is not inherent in the topic itself, in, say, "probability" or "calculus"; no one automatically broadens his or her mathematical education (*Bildung*) by simply reading a chapter in a math textbook. We must determine the *Bil-*

dungsgehalt, the "educational substance," of the topic, its potential as a "content of education," and this *educational* substance of a topic must be found by the teacher, for *this class* in *this place* in *this material*. Wolfgang Klafki (1995) offered an operational solution to the task of doing this in his epoch-making "Didactic Analysis," a paper that has been read by virtually every teacher in Germany. He formulated a set of five questions and several subquestions that represent "instructions" which, used judiciously, bring out the educational substance in the process of lesson planning. I will put the essence of his questions in my own words—Teachers should work out:

- How the topic represents the discipline, and which important field of human culture is opened up by it.
- What the topic's importance is for the present and future lives of the students.
- What the topic's structure is; this has to be evaluated in the context of discipline on the one hand and students' interests on the other.
- Which ways of learning and dealing with the topic in the classroom have to be provided.

Probability is, for example, undisputedly an important math concept, and there is no question that mastery of the ideas of probability opens up an important area of math. For students, this concept assumes a relatively trivial meaning when tossing a coin and in games of chance (for example, throwing dice). Its uses are less trivial in learning theory (trial and error), for example. As I explain in more detail in Chapter 7, one can easily imagine that first "throwing dice" and then discussing the outcomes will enable students to approach the topic—which is probability— quickly, and structure it in a useful way. This means the teacher in the math lesson I discuss in that chapter followed (in that case implicitly rather than explicitly) the lines of didactical planning which Klafki, in his turn, reconstructed for the use of German teacher education students.

4. Finally, there are the *teacher's* structuring and evaluating *activities*, which constitute the smallest units of classroom work. These activities are a complicated result of lesson planning, of awareness and interpretation of the students' interests and abilities, and of seemingly spontaneous decisions. Regarded from a didactical point of view the "method in't" is the students' *Bildung*: Teachers perceive, plan, and decide, guided by the idea of the students' Bildung. In other words, all measures they take are didactically legitimate insofar as they are intended to *build an adequate Weltbild*—take note of the etymology, *Bild*ung and Welt*bild*!—and to form able hands and minds.

As an example, let us consider the following excerpt from the lesson on "Throwing dice" that I will discuss in Chapter 7:

Teacher: . . . How many *different* outcomes do you think there are with two dice?
            (There follows a lot of hard thinking and pencil-and-paper work.)

David: Thirty-six. Six sixes. . . .Six goes with every number.
Teacher: . . . Do you mean I can have a six with a two, and a six with a one?
David: Yes.
Gary: Because there's six numbers on a dice and we have two dice. You can
            have a one with a two and keep on going. One three, one four, one five,
            one six. Then two one, two two,—
Ian: . . . I think it's sixteen. . . . Because . . . You're going to get six with one,
            aren't you? . . . So you've got all the other numbers. Then, er, the two.
            You're only going to get four different ones because, er, you have the
            rest in the six—in the one line.
Teacher: . . . Would you like to write them out [that is, on the blackboard]? Either
            the way David and Sally are talking or the way Ian has just been talking.
            Whichever way you think is—is best or right. (Martin, Williams, Wild-
            ing, Hemmings, & Medway, 1976)

In Table 2.2, I list all of the possible outcomes—and Gary's and Ian's solutions.
    One might think that "Ian's way of talking" is the right one—that depends on
the point of view. Either you *see* an *ordered* pair of dice, then {1;6} (for example,
a yellow dice showing "1" and a red one showing "6") is not equal to {6;1} (yellow "6" and red "1"), or order does not matter, which means that Ian is right. We
are not told how the teacher evaluates the results. What we do see is that the process is *constructed* by the teacher. The logic of this process, its method, is obviously not only found in the teacher's interest in a correct mathematical *Weltbild*,
but also in the students' ability to see things mathematically. The teachers' situa-
tionally embedded decisions are guided by an idea, which is conceptualized as *Bildung* in German Didaktik.

CONCLUSION

I have claimed that *Bildung* is the process in the course of which specific human
beings acquire what makes humans human. I have tried to show two different

TABLE 2.2.   Different Outcomes When Throwing Two Dice Simultaneously

6	1	5	1	. . .	2	1	1	1	
6	2	5	2	. . .	2	2	1	2	
6	3	5	3	. . .	2	3	1	3	
6	4	5	4	. . .	2	4	1	4	
6	5	5	5	. . .	2	5	1	5	
6	6	5	6	. . .	2	6	1	6	
Gary's line:		1	2	<>	2	1	(order matters)		
Ian's line:		1	2	=	2	1	(order does not matter)		

things. Firstly, the concept of *Bildung* has practical implications for teaching. It serves to establish the connection between the achievements of humanity and culture on the one hand, and the young people in a society who have to adopt this culture on the other.

In this context, secondly, it is not useful to speak about "instruction," pedagogy or "curriculum" in a general way; instead, we must distinguish the different areas of didactic reasoning. General statements tend to simplify matters; processes of arguing and deciding about specifics need different and differentiated ways of argument and criteria—for, say, the classroom and for, say, the political arena. With such differentiation, our conception of *Bildung* can be adjusted more precisely to the different didactical problems we are considering.

The following chapters pursue these themes.

3

General Didactics:
A Theoretical Framework

A GLANCE BACK INTO THE HISTORY OF
GERMAN DIDAKTIK

About 350 years ago, Johann Amos Comenius (1592–1670) demanded schools for everyone. In the words of the title of his main work (Keatinge, 1931, p. 17):

THE GREAT DIDACTIC
Setting forth
The whole Art of Teaching
all Things to all Men
or
A certain Inducement to found such Schools in all
the Parishes, Towns, and Villages of every
Christian Kingdom, that the entire
Youth of both Sexes, none
being excepted, shall
Quickly, Pleasantly, & Thoroughly
Become learned in the Sciences, pure in Morals,
trained to Piety, and in this manner
instructed in all things necessary
for the present and for

the future life,
in which, with respect to everything that is suggested,
Its Fundamental Principles are set forth for the essential
nature of the matter,
Its Truth is proved by examples from the several
mechanical arts,
Its Order is clearly set forth in years, months, days, and
hours, and, finally
An easy and sure Method is shown, by which it can
be pleasantly brought into existence.

In the text of *The Great Didactic*, published in 1656, Comenius developed a set of fundamental principles of teaching that covered:

- The reasons for the necessity of instruction for everyone
- The principles by which the field of what to know can be determined
- The rules which, if followed, ensure success in teaching

Comenius addressed teachers, but these teachers were, of course, different from the teachers we know today. His first "practical" task was to work out textbooks and a curriculum for his schools and the most famous of these texts was, of course, the *Orbis Sensualium Pictus* (The Circle of the World Insofar as It Can Be Perceived by Our Senses). As Comenius saw it, the *Orbis*, and the other similar texts he developed, provided what was necessary for the different phases of life and the corresponding schools—a curriculum in the strict sense.

Of course, schools and teacher education everywhere were to change dramatically in the centuries after Comenius's work. In Germany, for instance, the first *Lehrerseminare* (teacher training colleges) were founded about 100 years later, and another 100 years later these colleges had become the sole institution for the training of elementary school teachers. In the German tradition, Adolph Diesterweg (1790–1866) stands for this institution. His *Guide to the Education of German Teachers* from 1851 (1958) assembled the kind of knowledge he judged necessary for the, by then, clearly defined teaching profession: both the knowledge that was needed for the general education of teachers, and the knowledge that Diesterweg regarded as an essential tool for their teaching practice—a Didaktik in today's meaning of the term. Curiously, many of the rules and prescriptions he offered prospective teachers are virtually identical to those we found in Comenius's writing—in particular, their shared leitmotif: *Teach according to nature!*

There were many German teacher trainers, in addition to Diesterweg, who sought to codify the professional knowledge of elementary school teachers. And, in the course of the following 100 years, and to the present day, a culture around the production of such knowledge about classroom work and about how to organize it has developed: the German Didaktik.

Over the past 70 years, the training of elementary school teachers in Germany has become more and more academic and gradually aligned with the preparation and training of grammar school (*Gymnasium*) teachers. Comprehensive universities were established in the 1970s, and in these institutions all prospective teachers study in almost the same program irrespective of the type of school where they will teach later on. Parallel to this institutional development, knowledge about classroom work at school has not only increased rapidly, but has also become more detailed and more sophisticated. Didaktik has been elaborated to meet the demands of a scientific or research discourse.

But in the late 1950s when I studied education, the situation around Didaktik was quite unsatisfactory. There was an urgent need for an organization of the body of knowledge that had accumulated over the centuries. This need was acute in the case of teacher education; the students faced their first practical studies—and had to be prepared for this work. Both Wolfgang Klafki's (first published in 1962) famous essay on *Didaktische Analyse* (Didactic Analysis) and the—misleadingly—so-called "*lerntheoretisches Modell von Unterricht*" (model of teaching based on learning theory) that was developed by Paul Heimann (1970) and spread by Wolfgang Schulz, were drafted in this particular context. The ideas in both of these texts have served generations of prospective teachers in helping them to comprehend what they were to see in the school, and what they will have to cope with.

The next step in the postwar evolution of Didaktik was political rather than educational. In 1964, Georg Picht published a booklet with the alarming title *Die deutsche Bildungskatastrophe* (The Catastrophe of German Education). After noting the rapid increase of the population of West Germany, he predicted a serious lack of qualified manpower in general, and of teachers in particular. It seemed to him that, most importantly, the number of teachers had to be doubled by the 1970s in order to merely maintain the standard of the educational system.

Picht's plea was only one of the most striking voices in the concert involved in the fundamental dispute concerning the question of whether the West German educational system of that period was efficient. There were also the arguments that important democratic principles were not being implemented in the educational system; for instance, the participation of teachers, pupils, and parents; the accessibility of the administration to the public; equal-entry opportunities within the system; and so on.[25] A substantial increase in funds for the educational system and for educational research followed this concern, and the support of educational research led to an importation of theories, models, and findings from research abroad, and particularly from the Anglo-American countries—where it seemed there were answers to the questions and solution to the problems that we Germans seemed to have.

This search for solutions in the Anglo-American experience was highlighted with the publication in 1967 of Saul B. Robinsohn's project on *Bildungsreform als Revision des Curriculum* (Educational Reform as a Revision of the Curriculum).

This paper imported the term "curriculum" into the Federal Republic, and produced, as a result, an almost insurmountable body of literature and an extremely diverse set of realizations of curriculum, or *Lehrplan,* development. In this context, the taxonomy of educational objectives developed by Benjamin Bloom and his collaborators was also eagerly adopted. Its promoters promised that, by using this taxonomy, objectives could be derived more objectively. Institutionally, all the states in the Federal Republic created institutes, which in addition to the in-service training of teachers, also had the development of curricula as their objective.[26] Today, Robinsohn's approach has fallen into oblivion.

Herwig Blankertz confronted this same context, but he interpreted the situation in a different way. What he saw was a confused mixture of traces of the Didaktik tradition and attempts to modernize education—both the system and its theory. His famous *Theorien und Modelle der Didaktik* (Theories and Models of Didaktik); (1969) was his contribution—and we were enthusiastic about what he had done. His approach appeared to promise some order and, in addition, it seemed to do so using the theoretical positions of "research." *Theorien und Modelle der Didaktik* has been invoked again and again since its publication.

As it turned out, instead of serving as a guideline, Blankertz's analysis was often used as a replacement for Didaktik as a whole. But it was just the critical examination of didactical theory Blankertz had aimed at. Thus, stones were given to prospective teachers as bread. As a result, the best of our students are able juggle philosophical positions, but they became helpless in the face of classroom practice in the schools. And so they turned to recipes for practice—sometimes good and sometimes bad, at any rate age-old and not critically examined.

As I see it, the situation in German Didaktik today is like this. On the one hand, "theories and models of Didaktik" are still quite popular, but because they cannot help prospective teachers, there is an urgent need, on the other hand, for texts and discussions of Didaktik as such. At the end of their programs, my students always have difficulty organizing their observations and all the information they have about classroom work. Their difficulties grow when one recognizes that their task in the classroom does not mean teaching in general, but rather subject teaching and that, in addition to general didactics, they also take courses in subject matter didactics, that is, the Didaktik of teaching physics or German.

This is an unsatisfactory situation. Didaktik has come to resemble an overgrown garden: untrimmed, proliferating fruit trees; some flowers here and there showing the taste of former generations; and weeds everywhere. I am seeking to recultivate this garden here. To do this, I believe we need a theory:

- *On* the classroom in the school, which is intended
- *For* teachers, and which
- *Opens up* the field of their professional practice

I take the knowledge that has been collected in past centuries, and especially in the past decades, as a starting point. Then I try to recognize structures within this knowledge, in order to distinguish important matters from unimportant ones and to identify connections between things that on the surface of the Didaktik discourse seem to be separate. One can best find one's way in a broken area when looking at it from outside. So I am looking at the classroom—or even into the classroom—from society's point of view. Finally, I discuss in more detail those issues which turned out to be the significant.

THE OUTLINES OF CLASSROOM WORK AT SCHOOL

"Didaktik" describes knowledge *about classroom work in schools*.[27] What is the most general set of terms we can use to trace *classroom* work back to its irreducible core? I believe that these most general terms will start with something like this: Classroom work is the *passing on of culture within the context of the reproduction and the development of a society*. I will now give this elementary idea a coherent shape by offering a body of defining axioms. By "axiom," I mean a proposition that is immediately clear and, therefore, does not have to be proved—and is not provable anyway—but which can function as a basic principle for a theory.

As I see it, the following three axioms are sufficient for a theory of teaching:

1. *The axiom of culture*: In every society there is a *culture* that makes survival and social coexistence possible; this culture is a complement to the equipment that nature provides.
2. *The axiom of tradition*: In every society there is a *passing on* of culture; that is, the culture is transmitted from those who have acquired it to those who have not. (Or, the wheel is only invented once.)

The "passing on of a culture" does not imply any particular methods of passing on though, in fact, we only talk of "teaching" when the transmission is institutionalized, and takes place in a relatively stable, habitual, typical form. I express this in the next axiom:

3. *The axiom of institution*: The transmission of culture within a society is *institutionalized*.

Nota bene, this axiom is not an empirical statement—and, indeed, none of these axioms are; there are also noninstitutionalized forms of passing on. As an axiom in a theory of teaching, this third axiom simply means that we only talk of "teaching" when the passing on is institutionalized.

These three axioms are sufficient to circumscribe what we call in our language and culture "teaching" or "instruction"—in classrooms, seminars, and the like. In other words, what is said in axioms 1 to 3 *must be assumed* whenever we talk of teaching or instruction; and it is *only* the elements defined in these axioms that are needed to talk of teaching or instruction in general. We could base a general theory of "teaching" or "instruction," on this, or—to put it more precisely—we could develop a theory (in the figurative sense of the word) out of these axioms. Such a theory would cover religious instruction prior to marriage, or driver education, as well as classroom work at school.[28]

But in this book I am not discussing teaching in general. More specifically, I deal with classroom work in schools that everyone is required to attend; that is, classroom work at a school whose central purpose is the passing on of culture, and which is understood, moreover, to have a specific *educational task*. In order to define this educational task, additional axioms are required—and, of course, we have to introduce the concept of "education" to do this. The difference between those who know and those who do not know (that is, the second of the previously mentioned axioms) has to be rephrased as a difference between generations. Thus, we have:

4. *The axiom of generations*: In every society there is an *older generation* of those who are full members of this society, and a *younger generation* of those who are not yet full members of the society.

And this axiom leads to an objective, that is, to the *obligation* of the older generation toward the younger:

5. *The axiom of the minimum*: The older generation is responsible for the passing on of a *cultural minimum*.

When members of the younger generation have this minimum at their disposal, we call them "adults" and award them a majority in the legal sense of the term: We treat them as independent, mature, and responsible persons.

With these five axioms, all classroom work in the school seen as an educational organization is outlined. Summarizing, we could define classroom work in the following way: *Classroom work is the passing on a minimum of culture from (and by) the older generation to the younger one.* I prefer such an axiomatic definition, both to preclude essentialist statements and to avoid fruitless claims that classroom work *really* means this and that, or even something else.

With this the boundaries are set and the field is clear. Now we can ask what classroom work looks like on the inside. I use the very old method of dialectics; that is, I introduce differences, empirically relevant conceptual pairs, to obtain a more differentiated picture ("difference"—"differentiated": I have chosen this wordplay with care).

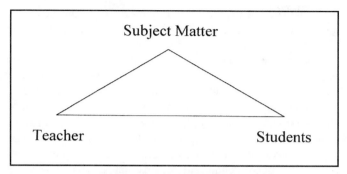

FIGURE 3.1.   The didactical triangle.

FROM SOCIETY TO THE CLASSROOM

Let me begin this exploration of classroom work from the inside with a more complete discussion of its three determinants as outlined in the axioms: *culture*, the *generation of adults*, and the *rising generation*. I will then turn to the "process."

German textbooks of Didaktik frequently begin with a discussion of the so-called "didactical triangle" (see Figure 3.1). Usually the discussion also ends at that point, the didactical triangle serving as either a definition or a heuristic model of classroom. My axioms locate the classroom *within* the larger context of *society* (see Figure 3.2). Why?

When looking into classrooms, we have to avoid the typical shortcomings that are a logical consequence of a society-free concept of "classroom":

- A focus on child-centeredness may lead to the splendid isolation of individual idiosyncrasies.
- A subject matter orientation may provoke a sense of alienation from "real life."
- A teacher-centered view may support authoritarian domination.

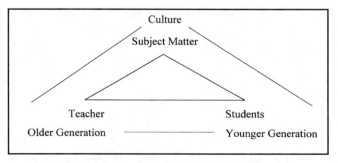

FIGURE 3.2.   The didactical triangle in its context.

Locating the classroom in society allows us to precisely define the respective roles and functions of actors and of subject matter and makes it possible to avoid both theoretical shortcomings as well as infringements in practice.

Thus, if we want to understand the meaning of "subject matter," we should not restrict our considerations to what in Germany has been traditionally called the "instructional content"; that is, what is worked on in classroom. Instead, we have to develop our understanding of the content of the classroom in terms of the culture as a whole. It is similar with "students" and "teachers." We all know the moralizing postulate that teachers and, especially, students should be seen as complete human beings. However, within the framework of a theory of classroom—in society—work we do not need such moralizing postulates: What "teachers" and "students" represent in the classroom must emerge from them being human beings *in human society*. So, in the next three sections, I follow the lines from the outer triangle of Figure 3.2 to the inner one of Figure 3.1, so to speak—from "culture," "older generation," and "younger generation" to "matter," "teacher," and "student." As I said before, I will do this by introducing significant differences.

CULTURE

When I speak of "culture," I am speaking of a culture as a whole and not of one of the proverbial "two cultures." The kind of understanding that sets "culture" against technology, science, or other unpleasant or merely useful things does not reach far enough. *What culture as a whole represents must be illustrated by contrasting "culture" and "nature"*: Culture is produced by humankind; it is material worked on and shaped. Nature on the other hand is what is required for such production: It is the material basis for a culture.

But it is not quite that easy to define "culture" by simply contrasting it with "nature." Whenever we look at a human being, we quickly realize that the limits are blurred. At every point at which we try to understand *in particular* what we call our "nature," we find that it is formed by the particular culture we live in; our "nature" is *cultivated*; it is a "second nature."

Thus, for a theory of classroom work, the simple comparison of "culture" and "nature" is unproductive. But it is didactically fruitful when we relate these two sides to one another: We call "nature" that which we regard to be presupposed to what we call "culture"; that is, as its material basis. From this point of view, human culture can develop into nature, and what we call "nature" can turn out to be a cultural product.

Instead of further philosophical discussions, let us look at a stretch of Germany's most beautiful, and in parts actually quite "unspoiled," example of nature: the *Lüneburger Heide* (the Lüneburg Heathlands). It is a product of culture, which is only preserved in what we admire as natural beauty by means of sound cultivation, helpful sheep and bees.

This may be enough to show what I mean by presupposing that it is the *entire culture* we have to think of when we think of classroom work. Let us now have a look at the differences.

The Products

On the one hand, we understand "culture" by *products*, particularly if they are present in the form of cultural monuments, books, and pieces of music, or in the landforms developed and cultivated by humans. On the other hand, by "culture" we also think of the process of producing, or of "cultivating" such products, and we think of their *producers*; that is, of human beings. *Human spirit* is kept in the *products;* we *interpret* them as documents of human spirit. Karl Marx (1953, p. 243) used a nice metaphor when he described the Great Industry as "the open book of *human faculties*, the human *psychology* that we can perceive with our senses." What thus makes a human being human becomes evident in the products of culture.

When I bring *"nature"* into these considerations, I come to a new aspect: What is the relationship between the humans who produce culture on the one hand and what we consider to be "nature" on the other? Generally it goes like this: Culture enables humankind to rule over nature and to meet fundamental needs; there are different ways of ruling over nature, which have been systematized as the "symbolic forms": from the Cave Paintings of Lascaux to the schematic drawings of its insides that came with my outboard motor. And there are different sectors of "nature" that are ruled: my inner nature, the "faculties of nature," the force that is set free by gatherings of people, and so forth. In other words, *culture is materialized in products that are produced to meet fundamental needs of humankind.*

The Producers

Let me now bring in the *producers* of culture. I will not consider this area in detail, but only draw attention to one aspect that is important for my later discussions and for that I will call the *anthropological syllogism*:

Humankind has produced culture.
I am a member of humankind, as are our students.
Therefore, in principle *we* are able to produce culture.

Obviously this concept is important when it comes to the acquisition and a productive further development of culture—which is the part of the younger generation.

The Ruling Culture

It would be ideological—in a bad sense—if we talked of "culture" and left it at that. Pierre Bourdieu and Jean-Claude Passeron (1973) have reminded us very clearly that it is the *ruling culture* that is handed down in the classroom; the "older generation" from my fourth axiom abstracts the political and economical constitution of the society which this term "older generation" represents.

This is the place for what we in Germany call curriculum theory (*Lehrplantheorie*). Weniger's curriculum theory from 1952, with its political analysis, remains the most adequate one, and has validity outside Germany, although the normative role he attributes to the state as the "regulating factor" in the dispute of interest groups in society may strike those outside mainland Europe as puzzling or misguided. But, while the role Weniger gives the state may be arguable, the question of what should be validly taught in school remains—the "cultural minimum" of the fifth axiom.

The counterposing of *ruling* and *oppressed* cultures is an important topos in both German and international didactic discussion. In the 1960s and 1970s, it was the lower social class in the Federal Republic of Germany that was attended to by Didaktik; today it is women, immigrants, and the handicapped. In this one can see very clearly that a mere juxtaposition of ruling and oppressed cultures has, so to speak, counterproductive consequences. These can be observed for instance in the success of programs for compensatory education (such as *Sesame Street*). They were designed to help lower class children and children belonging to nonruling cultures. But they have proved useful especially for middle-class children, who by definition belong to the ruling culture.

There is no way out when the issue of the cultural minimum is framed in this way, that is, in terms of *ruling* versus *oppressed.* But one can also understand this issue in a dialectical way and then, one piece at a time, work on it in classroom practice more or less like this: The claim to grasp *culture as a whole*, the totality of what makes human beings human, leads—when it is critically taken at its word—to subcultural traditions, which prove the ruling culture to actually be the *ruling* culture and not culture as such. So, for instance, in 1993 there was much ado about the "discovery" of America by Christopher Columbus—even in schools. Working on "Spain," "world trade," "navigation," and "discovery" in the classroom will lead inevitably, so to speak, to indigenous peoples and their miserable fates—if not, it was not the whole story that was being told and worked on.

Selection

The next problem on our way from society to classroom is the problem of *"selection from the ruling culture."* In Germany, the best-known solutions to this problem can probably be reduced to two:

■   The *reduction* of the whole; that is, "didactic reduction" by which the whole body of knowledge is "reduced" to a set of consistent ideas and facts that can be dealt with in a given course or grade; and to

- A *generalization* of the particular, the principle of the "exemplary" that is, working out a single item that represents the characteristic traits of a specific body of knowledge

Obviously each of these solutions presupposes the other: One cannot master the world from the particular without an idea of the whole; and every reduction is aimed at something particular, which exemplarily represents an integrated part.

We have arrived at the classroom. So, let us turn to the younger generation.

THE RISING GENERATION: STUDENTS

Even a brief glance at the standard writing on Didaktik reveals an astonishing observation: Virtually without exception, "students" appear in the abstract modality of "learning"—in analogy to teachers who appear in the modality of "teaching."[29] But when I introduced the idea of the "rising generation" in the fourth axiom, I was thinking of a complete specimen of the species *Homo sapiens sapiens*—the human being as a whole. So the question is *what makes a member of the younger generation a "student"?*

"Student" Versus "Human Being"

We all know the polemic that contrasts "student" with "human being "[30]: Susanna is "not only" my "student" whom I am to teach as her "teacher"—she "really is" an entire "human being" and ought to be regarded as such. For the moment, this is no more than a confusion of a definition and a pedagogical moral. "Student" merely is a definition according to the *genus proximum* and *differentia specifica* scheme; that is, a "student" is a "human being" (next species) which is attending school (specific difference). But we can look deeper into that difference.

One could think of the entire range of human possibilities and compare them with the selection that is accessible to the efforts made in classroom work. This is the reasonable argument underlying the *topos* of "merely cognitive classroom work," meaning that only cognitive educational objectives were being aimed at.

Or, one could take "humans" in their everyday life and point out that classroom work takes place within a protected area separated from everyday life. This, too, would be a reasonable argument in the reach of the opposition of "student" and "human." And perhaps there are additional possibilities. At least we may see that the opposites of "human" on the one hand and "student" on the other hand make it possible to get to didactically fruitful differentiations. But not only that! By introducing differences, we introduce specific aspects, or problems, into the framework of our theory. We locate *within* this framework what is very often isolated from its context—and is, therefore, discussed in a moralizing rather than in a theorizing way.

The Need for Education

When we think about young people, the question of being human also arises in another way. On the one hand, they are, as soon as they are born—in fact as soon as they are conceived—in principle and without any reservations specimens of the human species in its widest sense, and it is anthropology that unfolds their nature in this sense. On the other hand, they are obviously and *de* facto still *not fully educated* (or *fully uneducated*). We will probably find this difference symbolized in some way in every culture as two moments in the life of a person are emphasized: the moment of birth, and the moment of initiation into society.

In the Christian Church, God's mercy—and thus "being human"—is promised to the child directly after birth through christening. The child has to understand the importance of this in the course of growing up *and* education. The end of this process is symbolized in confirmation or similar initiation rites. After confirmation, the person is also, so to speak, empirically and legally a more or less completely educated member of the church, of society, a human being. I use this example for illustration, because the German theory of *Bildung*, with the help of which we understand a human being's development as his or her *educational career*, originates from this tradition.

"Subjective" Needs and Societal Demands

The not yet grown-ups have specific—"subjective"—interests or *needs*. These interests are opposed to societal *demands,* which are sometimes also called "objective needs"; such needs, which are thought to be their real needs, derive from their position in society. It is assumed that the young would want to have particular dispositions and abilities at their disposal—if they were aware of their real needs and if they were able to express them. But what if the supposed needs are not compatible with the interests, the natural equipment, the social orientations— with, in other words, the "subjective needs" of the young? Of course, here the way would be opened up to any kind of "ruling arbitrariness"—if the general pedagogical presupposition of the "independence of the pupil" was not in the way: The young ones have, and sometimes articulate, biographically conveyed, particular needs, which we interpret pedagogically as an expression of their aim for autonomy. That means that an acquisition of what society expects to be acquired is only possible if this can be linked to the *subjective needs.*

Starting from this notion of "subjective needs," we come to the same conclusion: "Subjective needs" is a construct describing motives of and for action. As soon as their content is verified, these subjective interests are interrelated to situations in which they are opposed by demands that can be interpreted as "offers." Even schools without a formal curriculum make an appropriate "offer" to their students. And, in addition, they make sure that their students make use of this offer in a particular way, so that, in the end, their students can participate in the predominant culture to the extent that is assumed to be necessary. In the language of psychology, the link between these two aspects, between the "subjective" and the "objective" needs, is well-known as "motivation."

Individual Ways

Let us now introduce the contrasting concepts of the *universal* and the *particular*. By this we are, on the one hand, introducing an awareness of the shaping of a common habit, and, on the other hand, of the development of an individual style. By giving an obligatory *general* education in the classroom possibilities for an *individual Bildung* are opened up to the young *by giving a specific character in the dimensions of the universal.*

A very simple example may serve as an illustration: In their first year at school, children learn standard handwriting; differences are considered as mistakes. A few years later every child writes in his or her own *individual* way. All manner of writing is accepted as long as it is *generally* readable.

Grouping of Students

Today it may seem remarkable that in discussions of didactics, "students" appear *in groups*, especially in "classes." This is only remarkable when one accepts that the often-quoted *topos* that puts the *individual* child exclusively at the center of pedagogical attention. But according to our fourth axiom, the term "student" stands for the species, more precisely for the rising generation. From this point of view, it would be more remarkable if it were individuals to whom culture is passed on.[31] When we have our eye on the "human being," the following generation is always defined collectively: as "the children of the Lord" within Christian tradition; or as "reasonable human beings," as specimens of "humankind," within the tradition of the Enlightenment.

In this respect it is not the collective forms of the students' existences in the classroom that need an explanation. Indeed, we can go on to ask why, and for what purpose, the rising generation is subdivided into individual units or subunits. What is the criteria for grouping students in classrooms? There are always socially relevant differences; that is, sex, age, membership of castes, classes, or subcultures. Above all, there are the differences in what we call "talent"—especially for those situations that are socially significant.

THE OLDER GENERATION: TEACHERS

As I have mentioned earlier, teachers usually appear in Didaktik only marginally as "teachers." This led to added arguments that seek to place teachers into their rightful positions as individuals and persons. So let us ask, what makes a person a "teacher"?

"Teacher" Versus "Human Being"

Setting "teacher" against "human being" also takes up a broad field in the Didaktik discussion—justifiably when it is meant as an effort to define the role of the "teacher." The teacher is, on the one hand, the *authority in society* who is competent and responsible for the passing on of culture. On the other hand the teacher is a *member of society*, of the older generation, and as such is, for instance, involved in the production and—sometimes—validation of knowledge (in its broadest sense) and thus in the discussion about its validity.

This preeducational difference has consequences for the classroom. As a member of society—as a "human being"—teachers have a standpoint in society, a position as well as point of view, and they have their images of the world (*Weltbild*), in which they find themselves. Accordingly teachers have a *specific interest* in every fact they teach. It is part of the professionality of at least modern teachers that they do not turn these interests into a stipulation of a teaching doctrine. But would their professionality lead to the denial of the fact that they are individual members of society, and complete "human beings"?

This contradiction disappears when we interpret it dialectically. Teachers are members of the older generation; they are involved in social debates, particularly in the fields in which they are specifically competent. And that is exactly *why* they are able to convey knowledge "competently"—as something that has grown, that is developing, and into which the rising generation is to be introduced.

"Teacher" or "Educator"

Another difference, or rather contrast, is firmly fixed in the German Didaktik, the contrast between the subject matter–oriented teacher, and the child-centered teacher, or the difference between "teacher" and "educator." Of course, this is not meant in its empirical but in its prescriptive sense: A teacher *should* not only be a "teacher" but also an "educator," just as the "child" *ought* to be the focal point of education.

This contradiction can also be explored in a constructive rather than a moralizing way. Let us take the standpoint of the subject-centered experts. They know that their obligation is the passing on of culture. They see their task as that of passing on valid and significant knowledge. But what if their knowledge is either not so clearly perceived or not accepted by those they are teaching? They always have to make sure that their *knowledge* is communicated in a way that makes it accessible and acceptable by the *students*. Likewise, the child-centered pedagogues *are* more than that when they really want to focus on the children's needs. What else do they do with the children beyond working on *matter* that is significant for the *students*! And, what is the significant knowledge? It is the knowledge that is indispensable for their pupils' upbringing in society.

THE PROCESS

Classroom work occurs in time. It is described by the actions carried out by the persons involved, and by the *patterns* of such actions. But, before we consider the classroom as a process, I have to make an important distinction that is too often lost. Teaching and classroom work, in particular, has to be distinguished from the *preparation* of teaching. In the Didaktik tradition, the preparation of teaching has pushed itself into the foreground—so much so that the "classroom" is presented almost solely from the standpoint of teachers' planning and lesson-giving. Fair enough! But the practice of the preparation of teaching is not the classroom as a whole. Both preparation for teaching and the subsequent evaluation must be distinguished from classroom work itself. Thus, the "theory of classroom" must not be confused with a theory of, let me say, the "strategy of the teacher's acting."

Informing and Reception

Let us first connect the second axiom of "tradition" with the fourth axiom of "generation." This implies that there is a difference between a state in which the rising generation does not possess a particular area of knowledge, and a later state in which they do possess that knowledge. Within the framework of the curriculum, teachers determine the knowledge required for bridging this gap, and they make it available for their students. Therefore, *informing* by the teacher, and *reception* by the student, represent the bottom line of the process—and in this exact order. At the end the students are *tested* to ensure that they have the knowledge at their disposal that is assumed to be necessary (according to the fifth axiom).

In this statement, I have not said one word about the immense range for possibilities of realizing given patterns in particular classrooms. And I will not evaluate specific realizations; that is, specific methods of organizing classroom work. What I am aiming at is a set of basic concepts—which in turn may serve as terms of speaking about, and even evaluating, classrooms.

Articulation

Using this framework, I can now develop the *logic of the process*. In general the *starting point* is given in the form of a *task* or a *problem*. From the perspective of the work to be done in the classroom three things are accomplished by the problem or task:

- A consciousness of being *ignorant*, or not being able, is conveyed: The problem cannot be solved with the students' knowledge; if they want to solve this problem or complete this task, they have to acquire new knowledge, or at least reorganize their knowledge.
- The problems and tasks of classroom work appear as a *symbolic equivalent* to the tasks that have to be solved in everyday life, in the present and the future.
- A *unit* of classroom work is defined: the span between the initial problem and its final solution, as it were. This unit is irreducible in the sense that all kinds of verbal "moves," or other activities, make sense only as part of this work.

Mostly the task is preceded by a recapitulation of what has been worked on before. So, this step serves—in the logic of the process—to remind the workers of the tools that are already available to them.

The *next step* is *working on the problem*, which has two aims:

- The problem should be solved.
- As they work on the problem, the (classroom) workers acquire competence and skills that have not been available to them before.

While typically there is not just one way of solving a problem, there must be somebody who knows at least one way. If this were one of the pupils it would be nice. But the institution of the classroom is based on the presupposition that the students do *not* know—for if they did they would not need instruction. There have to be teachers, whether they are, as is usually the case, present in person or whether they have metamorphozed into a means the pupils are working with, like Montessori's materials or the Internet. Above all it is the teachers, and only the teachers, who are able, in principle, to judge whether the product of the work is a *valid* solution (in the sense of the first axiom) to the problem that has been posed at the beginning of the lesson.

In a *further step*, the newly achieved abilities are—often—*applied* to similar, frequently more general, problems. Thus, three aims can be pursued:

- The students may practice their new abilities.
- The teacher may examine whether the proposed solution can be generalized. Can the technique be used for solving other problems?
- The application may also serve as a control as to whether the classroom workers (that is, the students) have actually achieved the promised skills.

The first two aims are optional. However, the control of success in learning is a necessary step in the process. The class has achieved its purpose and aim only when the pupils have left the state of ignorance and have, in fact, entered the state of knowing. Didactically interpreted, tests of any kind serve to ensure knowledge, attitudes, and abilities.

The Reception of Knowledge

Informing, taken literally, evokes the image of a *tabula rasa*, the plain wax tablet of antiquity onto which knowledge was to be carved, or that of the *Nürnberger Trichter*.[32] And for a course as a whole—not for the specific classroom situation—the idea of a *tabula rasa* is not really as inappropriate as progressive pedagogues make it appear. As long as we know no better (and are unwilling to hold a particular piece of genetic equipment responsible for intelligent, moral, or artistic behavior) we logically have to start with informing *as if* our students were a *tabula rasa*.

But we have to look at this from yet another point of view. Plato's Socrates compared informing with recollection: The teacher, like a midwife, has to get knowledge out of a human being, knowledge that is already inside the student—because it was acquired in a former life. Socrates' partners were adults. Obviously grown-ups—and growing-ups—are not inexperienced, at least at the time when they enter the classroom. They have a wide and differentiated knowledge at their disposal. At the beginning of their school lives, they have the knowledge they learned in their "mother's school." Later there is the knowledge that was imparted to them in earlier classes—as well as what they have learned in everyday life. They can, and they do, explicitly recall this knowledge. Recollection *is* an element of the informing: It is to link the knowledge at hand with knowledge that should be achieved. But, recollection in this sense does *not* take the place of informing. Fundamentally new knowledge cannot emerge from existing knowledge.

The *reception of knowledge* by the student is the counterpart of the informing. Again, this is a somewhat misleading formulation. The concept of the *Nürnberger Trichter* may be a nice image for this, but it actually does not fit the object it describes, and it does not do so, again, for logical reasons. I refer to the basic axioms and the discussion of "culture" in Chapter 2. What has to be passed down is, as I have suggested, something that has been produced by human beings. That means that the content of classroom work refers to the process of producing culture. Thus, work—in classroom and on culture—corresponds to production—*in* society and *of* culture. From this point of view, we may say: "Classroom work" has to be seen as *an equivalent*, or correspondent, *of "work" in society*; that is, *of the process of producing culture. Classroom work* is undertaken on the outcomes of the *societal work* retained in the cultural product that is being worked on.

Furthermore, the cultural products are present in class by means of a symbolic codification. To give an example:

> In 1765, James Watt invented the steam engine. This innovation improved the conditions of life in England enormously and made England one of the leading nations from the point of view of industrialization. As we know, inventions such as the steam engine initiated, or at least supported, modern capitalism and everything connected with it.

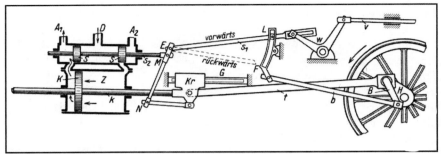

Source: Grimsehl, 1950, p. 104

FIGURE 3.3.   The steam engine.

I remember my lessons in physics some 50 years ago, or Alexander's lessons some 15 years ago. The steam engine was introduced in the way seen in Figure 3.3—a symbolic representation. The next step was the balance of energy. Figure 3.4 (of the Carnot circle process) is a model of the Second Theorem of Thermodynamics which goes like this: "In a closed system the amount of entropy will increase" (as in Figure 3.5). Both, figures and the words of the theorem, symbolize what happens within Watt's engine. This is physics. And this is one representation—from a variety of other possibilities—of "steam engine in the late 18th century." In our physics lessons we worked on these representations.

One of the different representations of "steam engine in the late 18th century" may be a story, in strict sense, of a Birmingham family at that time. Representations of this kind were the stuff of history. And in the history classroom, the concepts used in interpreting the family's story were not "vapor" or "energy" but "wealth and poverty," "pollution," "rate of mortality," "steel production," and "revolution," and the like.

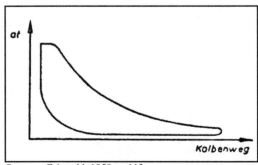

Source: Grimsehl, 1950, p. 112

FIGURE 3.4.   The Carnot circle process.

$$\eta = \frac{T_1 - T_2}{T_1}$$

FIGURE 3.5.   The Second Theorem of Thermodynamics.

Thus, work in class is not identical with the work of, for example, James Watt or the handiwork of the English craftsmen in my example. In the classroom we are dealing with a quite specific work—work with and on symbols. This work with and on symbols is *interpretation*, the analysis of that which is embedded in the subjects of (classroom) work, especially of their meaning.

But, actual classroom work is still more complicated than my formulation—that classroom work is interpretation of symbols—suggests. Let me give another example: When I was a student, we had to translate scenes from Shakespeare's *Julius Caesar* from English to German. There are (and were then) fine translations of *Julius Caesar* available. Why add other translations (and they were not very good) to that famous assembly? But the point of our exercises as pieces of classroom work was not the product itself, that is, the translation and interpretation of *Julius Caesar*. Instead, our classroom products were significant as (and as long as we believed that they were) documents, as points in a *Bildungsprozess,* a process of growing into one's own self, a process of intellectual and moral development.

The Separation of Classroom and Life

I now introduce another difference: the difference between "life" and "classroom." A well-known progressive argument goes like this: "Classroom work" is meant to prepare for life, and, therefore, it is *life* itself which ought to be worked on and acquired in class, and not symbols which at best stand for life. But the specific achievement of "classroom work" really lies in what the "progressive" criticism so often objects to: Classroom work—be it "traditional" or "progressive"—provides control over those forces that would overwhelm adolescents in everyday life, if they were left to their own devices. In the streets, for instance, they could learn about urban life but they could also learn how to become a prostitute or a heroin addict. In other words, "classroom work" takes place within intentionally narrow borders. However, those borders do not have their origins in arbitrariness of definition or the malice of authoritarian didacticians but rather in the *logic of a specific practice.*

The power of the progressives' objection to the separation of the classroom from life lies in a different place: There are degrees of closeness to the life in society that classroom work—activity and subject—refers to, and that it prepares for. This would seem to be a strong argument in favor of criticism of the separation between classroom work and real life. But this is an empirical argument and not a theoretical one! It is an argument against a particular organization of classrooms in a particular school—and not against the classroom as an institution.

The Outcomes

Let us now look at the end of the classroom process. As I have suggested, a test at the end of a lesson, a unit, or a course is obligatory. Such testing is focused on the question of whether it is really the valid culture (according to the fourth axiom) that has been acquired. Here, two situations have to be distinguished:

- In the classroom, the teacher has to check that the product of the classroom's work is of *appropriate quality*. But this does not guarantee that the producers (that is, the students), have achieved the competence they are striving for.
- This is why they are regularly put into a problem-solving situation similar to their classroom situations—but with a difference: In these situations, (that is, in the test situation), they are asked to prove that they are now *capable* of solving the task independently. When they show that they are able to do this, we conclude that they have acquired the knowledge and the abilities they ought to have. At this point, this piece of classroom work is at its end.

Acting Humanely?

I now take a further step, over and above "classroom work." Let us suppose that a piece of classroom work attained its aim, that the students who experienced it were competent. Unfortunately, that certification of competence does not guarantee that they would act humanely, for example, in accordance with the norms prevailing in society. Josef Derbolav has been one of the very few German didacticians to explore this problem—as he phrased it, the problem of the "dialectics of knowledge and conscience" (*Dialektik von Wissen und Gewissen*).

The problem of knowledge and conscience is, indeed, dialectical; every attempt to clear it up inevitably results in a practical disappointment—when, for example, the now grown-ups use their acquired knowledge to dismantle the culture that has been passed on to them for preservation and further development. (I think, for instance, of computer programming and the invention and dissemination of computer viruses.) Derbolav explored how to use the dialectic of knowledge and conscience for the good of teaching practice, and I will return to this theme in Chapter 8. Here, I only bring up one aspect of this issue.

Classroom work *has* its limits; that is, the classroom itself. This may sound odd. But classroom work ends where adult life begins; and in adult life it is each person's knowledge, orientations, and skills that ought to guide the search for responsible action. When it comes to directing and limiting these actions, didactics is at its end: *It is politics that must take up this responsibility.*

ON THE TEACHING OF SUBJECTS

Up to this point I have been exploring the classroom as such: its logic, its actors, the matter, and the process. But we have not come to an end yet. It is not "knowledge" in general that forms the basis for classroom work but *specific* knowledge; and it is not an abstract "conscience" that concerns us, but one that has to go into action in *particular* situations. So, we have to go one step further, to a discussion of the teaching of what we call "subjects," that is, to *subject matter didactics.*

The conception that underlies the idea of subject teaching is quite simple and we can capture it with one additional axiom:

6.   *The axiom of disciplines*: Culture is structured according to *fields* and society can be seen as subdivided into *subsystems.*

The subsystems of any society correspond to segments of the culture with distinguishable systems of practice, whether we take the ancient university "disciplines," of medicine, jurisprudence, theology; or the school "subjects," mathematics, mother tongue, art; or we think of the three Rs of elementary school. These "subjects" and the knowledge constituted within their limits all correspond to distinguishable systems of human social practice. Insofar as these subjects are treated in the classroom they are all alike. And there are—didactical—problems they all have in common. I will only name some of the problems that can be assumed to be significant for the practice of teaching of any of the subjects. Once more I will introduce these "subject matter problems" by introducing differences.

Such problems are:

■   The subject *as such* versus the subject within *the whole* of the subjects: Which side of that which makes a human being human is disclosed by *this* subject and by *only* this subject
■   The way, the method of acquiring the cultural segment in question: in accordance with *everyday experience* versus in accordance with a corresponding *science*, to name only the extremes
■   The way of processing the knowledge in a course: appropriate to the *genesis of knowledge* in the historical process of its accumulation versus appropriate to the *system* of a corresponding *discipline*

And looking at the young generation, whose members are taking their places in society:

■   The relevance of the matter: as determined within *culture* (for example, within the structure of a discipline) versus within the horizon of the *adolescents*
■   The status of a matter in *everyday life* versus in the *classroom* and so on

These are problems that are empirically significant for each and every subject. But they must also be discussed for each and every *specific subject.*

CONCLUSION

What I have outlined in this chapter limits the field that a theory of the classroom has as its object and, within these limits, yields a structured, differentiated map (that is, a topography) of the field. But important things are still missing.

Persons who know what the "classroom" really is still do not know how to teach. To fill in this gap the textbooks of "Didaktik" offer general "didactical principles" such as, "Teach (or educate) according to nature!" There are, of course, a variety of such recommendations about how to act in classrooms. What are such principles and precepts useful for?

At the beginning of this chapter, I referred to the didactical triangle. After considering the elements of the triangle, we have to place the relationships between these determinants in a particular way, for instance, the relationship between teachers and students. Take, for example, one principle, "Orient to the child," which is typically asserted quite nondialectically in the didactics for the elementary school. This principle can be interpreted as expressing an opposition to a rigid orientation toward society and its needs, as in my earlier discussion the student's "needs" and "interests."

In the same vein, what can be said about recommendations for ways of acting in the classroom? Specific recommendations, for example, approaches to "effective teaching," are probably not part of an outline of a didactical theory, but they are not worthless either. "Recommendations for acting" are those pieces of advice that say that one should act in a particular way, and only in this way, in this particular situation. The pedagogical situation is always (and in principle) open, and must be seen as open—that is the theoretical point of view. But teachers in their classrooms have to act. Every action, for example, the choice of a teaching method, the answer to a question, "closes" a situation that was open, and that was seen as open before it was closed.

Recommendations are relevant for this process of transforming a dialectically seen and open situation into a specific action, that is, a *practical* solution to the—dialectically formulated—problem. Advisers or instructors recommend (or require) a *specific* way of acting—knowing the range of *possible* solutions to the problem. Didactics can convey this *knowledge,* but the *problems* have to be solved in practice. A nondialectical use of "didactic principles," for example, "teacher-proof curricula," or "do it this way" does not necessarily lead immediately to bad teaching. But it does restrict those who follow the way it recommends as the only way; it advises a particular way of acting. Theory—didactics—should show a way *out* of such restrictions.

4

Can We (and What Can We) Learn from the History of Education?

This chapter has two parts. In the first part, I will present some pictures from the history of instruction; in the second part, with this history in hand, I will offer my answers to two questions: What do we mean when we say "We can learn from history"? And, is it possible to learn from history?

SOME PICTURES FROM THE HISTORY OF INSTRUCTION

In Umberto Eco's well-known novel *The Name of the Rose,* there is a subplot, the controversy between the delegates of the pope and of his antagonist, the Holy Roman emperor. Within the one, the "Catholic," the all-encompassing Church of that time, there were different ideas about how to handle worldly goods or terrestrial power. To that point in history, the easiest way to come to a decision had been made use of—to declare the dissident a heretic and burn him or her. But in this case the much more humane method of the ancient Greeks was applied, which was being restored to favor in the teaching practices of the universities that were being founded at that time: I mean the *Aristotelian dialectic.*

Instruction according to this method may have proceeded in the following way (Henningsen, 1974, pp. 46–47):

> *Quaeritur si* [It is asked if]: Charity, once possessed, can be lost again.
> *Scriptura dicit* [The Scriptures say]: Love will never come to an end (1 Cor. 13, 8).
> *Item* [Likewise]: If they had belonged to us, they would have stayed with us (1 John 2, 19). The source of your water be yours forever, and no stranger joined you.
> *Ad exponendum* [in order to explain] who is a stranger he says: Strangers are those who will hear: I don't know you.
> *Ex his videtur* [It is seen from this] that David had never possessed God's love before he sinned; and Judas hadn't either.
> *Sed contra dicit Scriptura* [But against this the Scriptures say] that the spirit of the Lord had been turned to David from the beginning (1 Kings 16, 13). So if he had the Spiritus Domini, he had His love as well, because the Spiritus sanctus is never without love.
> *Item* the Lord said to Judas while he was still with the Apostles that "because your names are enrolled in heaven" (Luke 10, 20) they will have the eternal life, so that, when they died, they would be saved—what would not be possible without charity [that is, His love] . . . .
> *Videtur inde* [It is seen then] that it is reasonable to say that even the damned participate in His love, and that His love, once possessed, is lost, and if it is lost, it can be restored.
> *Ad quod dicimus* [About this we say] (. . . you have to interpret the authority this and that way. . .) in order to gain salvation one must confess and bitterly repent one's sins.

The structure of the whole argument is given in Table 4.1.

There is, of course, the argument of the teacher at the end. But to that point the authorities, the Holy Bible, the Fathers of the Church, and the ancient philosophers, had all been consulted, the pros and cons of the matter weighed, and *sic et*

TABLE 4.1. Sic et Non

Quaeritur si . . .	**question**
	Scriptura dicit . . . argument: pro (and authority)
	Item . . . another argument: pro
	Ad exponendum . . . explication (for example, of a term)
Ex his videtur . . . conclusion—**sic**	
	Sed contra dicit Scriptura . . . arguments: contra
	Item . . .
	Item . . .
Videtur inde . . . conclusion—**non**	
	Item . . . another argument: contra
Ad quod dicimus . . . **solution** (decision) . . . by strengthening one group of arguments—either the pros or the cons—and destroying the other.	

non discussed. This was a great art. It was developed and mastered so brilliantly that it could even be reduced—playfully—to absurdity:

> "Are the cattle driven to the market held by the farmer or by the rope?" And the origins of an ancient joke are found in those days: "What you haven't lost, you've got; you haven't lost horns, so . . . ." (Henningsen, 1974, p. 44.)

In these last years of the Middle Ages, standards and patterns for teaching were set for future generations, no matter whether they developed the art of teaching by means of this dialectic further or criticized it vehemently (as, for instance, the Renaissance humanists did).

Other developments at the close of the Middle Ages were also of great significance for the history of instruction at school. But, before we consider these developments, let us have a look at another picture of a school. In a contract concluded in 1425 it says:

> The mayor, the judges, and the council of the city of Wesel have taken Master Albert van der Heggen from Nimwegen as their schoolmaster and have given to his charge the school of Wesel. It is his duty to teach and to instruct the children as a good schoolmaster owes it to his pupils, as he thinks it does the city and himself credit, and as he thinks it best for the children and the pupils. Moreover, he has to take the pupils to church and to other places where they should sing as it has always been done in Wesel. For his living he is allowed to take the same amount of money from the children as the schoolmasters before him did . . . . If anybody else in the city opens a school to teach boys, the council will at once prohibit him from doing so, because nobody else is in charge of the boys' school in Wesel but the before-mentioned Master Albert. (Michael & Schepp, 1973, pp. 51–52)

What might this school in Wesel have looked like? Perhaps like the school we see in Figure 4.1 which, of course, is a stylization. In any case, the children probably learned the three Rs and became familiar with everything a townsperson of those days needed to know. But even if this was only a little in terms of what we would think of as the knowledge that has to be taught in the school, it still represented skills that only a few had access to—and as such they were important skills. This contract, and many other documents, give evidence of the townspeople's strong wish for a minimum of skills and understanding, at a time when the cities were securing greater economic and political power in relation to the aristocracy and the clergy.

Martin Luther was part of this tradition, but he gave it a specific theological foundation. As he said in his famous treatise of the *Liberties of a Christian*, only educated people could assert these liberties (Luther, 1925). In consequence, that meant *education for all*. Following this Reformation tradition, the Bohemian Brethren, a Protestant Christian denomination in Catholic Hapsburg Bohemia, undertook the task of religious instruction in their mother tongue so that their

Source: Alt, 1960, p. 351

FIGURE 4.1.   A picture of a school in the Middle Ages.

members could become familiar with and defend their Christian doctrine against both the Catholic Church's interpretations of the Bible and the power and privileges of the clergy. Originally, this task was, as it had been in Luther's day, the duty of each paterfamilias, the father of each extended family (see Figure 4.2).

Source: Alt, 1960, p. 296

FIGURE 4.2.   A Bohemian Brethren family.

But, over time, more and more schools were established by the Brethren, a testament to their success in secular occupations.

I introduce this detail of the ecclesiastical history here because of the Brethren's last bishop, Jan Amos Komensky, better known by his Latin name Johann Amos Comenius, who became one of the most influential figures in the history of education. Above all, he was the first to successfully organize all the knowledge that humankind had accumulated and to turn it to the didactical purpose outlined in the title of his famous *Didactica Magna* (see Chapter 3). His famous reading book— or to be more exact, his language-picture-textbook—the *Orbis Sensualium Pictus*, is a telling example of his method and one of the classics of education. In this book the world, the circle (*orbis*) of Creation, is expressed symbolically—in words and pictures, with the words explaining the pictures. Thus, *the world becomes teachable*, a proposition I will explore in more detail in Chapter 9. Here let me give just one example from the central part of his book, the "parental status"; that is, the family. I will not translate the "story"; readers may find their own *words* for the *things* presented in Figure 4.3.[33]

Comenius's original frame of reference was the family in an early bourgeois community as Figures 4.2 and 4.3 depict it. From the seeds of this community, Comenius derived his idea of schools for *all*.

Societas Parentalis.

Conjuges, fulcipiunt
:x benedictione Dei)
ibolem (Prolem)
:fiunt Parentes.
Pater 1 generat,
Mater 2 parit
ilios 3 & Filias, 4
(liquando Gemellos.)
Infans 5
volvitur Fasciis, 6
ponitur in Cunis, 7
natre
Statur Uberibus, 8
nutritur Pappis. 9
Deinde,incedere di-
rperastro, 10   (scit
sit Crepundiis, 11
fari incipit.
Crescente ætate,
etati 12
Labori 13 adsuefit,
castigatur 14
non sit morigerus.
Liberi debent
rentibus
ultum & Officium.
Pater,
stentat Liberos,
borando. 15

Die Eheleute/ bekomen
(durch Gottes Segen)
Kinder/
und werden Eltern.
Der Vater 1 zeuget/
die Mutter 2 gebieret
Söhne 3 uñ Töchter/4
(zuweilen auch Zwillinge.)
Das kleine Kind 5 (6
wird gewickelt in Windeln
gelegt in die Wiege/ 7
von der Mutter
geseuget mit dē Brüsten/ 8
und ernehret mit Brey
([Muß.] 9
Darnach lernet es gehen
im Gängelwagen/ 10
spielt mit Spielgezeug/ 11
und hebt an zu reden.
Wañ es älter wird/ (12
wird es zur Gottesfurcht
uñ Arbeit 13 angewöhnet/
und gestäupet 14
wann es nit folgen wil.
Die Kinder/sind schuldig
den Eltern/
Ehre und Dienst.
Der Vater/
ernehret die Kinder
mit Arbeiten. 15

Q 3   Societas

Der Eltern Stand.

FIGURE 4.3.   "Elternstand," from Comenius's *Orbis Sensualium Pictus* (1978, pp. 244–245).

This brings me back to Luther again. Whether he really was the "father of the elementary school" (*Volksschule*), as we Germans tend to call him, remains an open question. However he is important for the history of teaching and instruction as the author of the *Smaller Catechism*. One of his achievements was his adaptation into German of the Latin liturgy of the Roman Catholic mass for the reformed church. And, as he wrote in his treatise on the "German Service" (*Deutsche Messe*):

> What the German service really needs is a plain and simple catechism. I am thinking of a set of questions and answers that could be used for the religious instruction of heathens who want to become Christians. It would have to teach them the dos and don'ts and what they need to know about Christianity. . . . There are three main pieces that tell us briefly and clearly what a good Christian needs to know: the Ten Commandments, the Creed, and the Lord's Prayer. (Luther, 1925, p. 297)

He added the doctrines of baptism and communion, and the five pieces that resulted made up his *Smaller Catechism*—a Christian's "core curriculum." Luther furthermore imagined a method of teaching this fundamental knowledge:

> The first question should be: "What do you say for your prayers?" Answer: "The Lord's Prayer." What does it mean, "Our Father, who art in Heaven?" Answer: "That the Lord is no earthly being, but our Heavenly Father, who will save us when we have died." "What do you understand by 'Hallowed be thy Name'?" Answer: "That we shall honor His name so that it will not be defiled." "But how is the Lord's name desecrated and defiled?" Answer: "If we who are His children do evil, teach evil and believe in evil." And so forth: "What do we mean by 'Thy kingdom'? How will it come? What is the Lord's will? What does 'our daily bread' mean?" etc. The same should be done with the Creed—"Who do you believe in?" "I believe in God, the Father Almighty," etc.—as well as with the Ten Commandments. (p. 298)

In the course of time, the teaching method seen here became a method of religious instruction named *catechisatio,* the catechetical method. We see this method in the practice of the Pietist August Hermann Francke (1663–1727), another important figure for the history of instruction and education in Germany. One of his students wrote down such a catechism (Nebe, 1927, pp. 2–8; my emphasis added):

> Francke's repetitions of his sermons had . . . created a great stir . . . . They not only attracted the children with whom he went through the sermon, but their relatives as well.
>
> On Sunday nights the early morning sermon is repeated step by step; on Mondays the same is done with the Sunday afternoon sermon.

Then follows an example, taken down word-for-word:

Francke then began to question the boys and girls on the early morning sermon. He addressed his questions to all of them, but, depending on the questions' degree of difficulty, either all children answered, only a few, or only one or two of the older ones who used to take down notes during the sermons. The first question was:

Question 1: Where was the introduction to the sermon taken from?

Answer: From the letter of Paul to the Colossians, chapter 2.

After a boy had read out loud the first seven verses of this chapter, Francke confirmed and explained the answer. Then he asked:

Q.2: What does Paul mean by "exertions"?

A: His prayers for the Colossians. Confirmation and explanation. Correct.

But since it was not Paul himself who planted that church, he was worried that they might stray from true faith to seek vain wisdom. Further down we find the following revealing passage:

Q.11: What characteristics do the children of the devil possess?

A: Committing sins. Explanation . . .

Q.12: But do the children of God not sin at all?

A: Here, some of the children say yes, others say no; Francke *criticizes them gently, and puts the question in different words:*

Q.13: Do the children of God sin voluntarily?

A: Of course not. Explanation. Correct. They don't commit sins intentionally.

The following sequence is remarkable, too:

Q.21: Which topics of the gospel were subject of today's sermon? . . .

Q.22: In which parts was the subject dealt with?

A: We talked about . . .

Explanation: Well done. Remember what you heard , think about it again, *so that you can make good use of it.*

Let me finally quote two questions that deal with measures against seduction:

Q.54: How do we have to apply a certain measure?

A: We have to seek God with all our hearts.

Q.55: Yes, but be more exact!

A: We have to examine ourselves thoroughly.

Explanation: Correct. The false prophet has to be sought out *in ourselves;* if it wasn't for him, we'd be invulnerable to all kinds of seduction.

The catechism ends after the repetition of the entire sermon and is followed by prayer, hymn, psalm, and closing hymn.

There is a constant formal pattern in this catechetical method of teaching: the question-answer-explanation pattern that we know all too well. This pattern underlies the instruction, aiming at developing ideas that are in the students' minds. But the examples I have selected tell us more than that; they reflect:

- An acknowledgement and consideration for the children's intellectual capacities; that is, Francke puts his questions in other, namely in easier words, in case the children failed to *understand*.
- Detailed requests to think about the content of the sermon so that *good use* can be made of it.
- The turn from outer behavior to *inner motives*.

We have to bear in mind that Francke's catechism was preceded by the sermon—the subject matter of the instruction so to speak—which was then "developed" in the example. But even without these hints we readily identify this social situation as "teaching" or "instruction" *in the modern sense of those words,* even if it seems primitive.

The catechetical method as it was developed by Francke and his collaborators shows that the pattern is flexible and not restricted to the essentials of the Christian faith; it can be applied to other topics as well. What other topics? I would answer: to everything that is imperative for life in the present and the future world—as, for example, Comenius set them out in his *Orbis Pictus.*

But let us not talk only about Comenius and Francke. About two generations after Francke, at the beginning of the 1770s, Johann Bernhard Basedow, a member of the "philanthropists," an informal group of progressive and enlightened educators of that time, attempted to improve the education of students of theology. Like Francke before him, Basedow endeavored to prepare the students for their future

**FIGURE 4.4.   The first copperplate print from
Basedow's *Elementarwerk* (1909, Tab. I).**

occupation as teachers in the church and school and, to do this, he prepared his famous *Elementarwerk* (Elementary Work).

Let us consider the first of the copperplate prints in this work (see Figure 4.4). These illustrations were complemented by a complete book of instructions for parents and private tutors from which the following dialogue is taken.

> Would you like to have a look at the copper plates?
> I'd love to, but you don't often give me the permission to do so. You always lock them up, so that I can't look at them when I want to. Why do you do that?
> If I let you look at them whenever you felt like, you would soon get tired of them; you wouldn't be able to enjoy them any more, just as you wouldn't delight in a good meal when you aren't hungry. Do you understand what I'm trying to say?
> No, not really. You are saying too much at a time.

This is as teacherly, as "didactic," as it can be.

> Mother. Here I have one of the pictures, the first plate. Let's have a look at it for a quarter of an hour.—Ah, I'd like to do that,
> Count the people!—One, two, three, four, five, six, or 1, 2, 3, 4, 5, 6.
> How many children are there?—Let me count them, 1, 2, 3, 4.
> What is the mother doing?—She is nursing the child.
> What can you tell from her face?—That she loves her baby very dearly. She is looking at it very tenderly.
> What is the maid doing?—She is feeding this boy.
> What is the boy on the right doing?—He is eating a piece of cake.
> What would the little girl behind the maid like to have?—She'd like to have the bun she's reaching for.
> I can see three fish, can you see them too?—I can see one on the hook, another one is lying on the table, and a third one is lying on the floor.
> Can you see the fruits too? --Not yet, but now I can see some in the basket. I would ask for some, but they are only pictures. (Basedow, 1965, pp. 211–212)

This is highly developed teaching art. The catechetical method was becoming more sophisticated and a large number of documents from that period show that it was being employed, and employed excellently, to help children understand what they experienced, observed, or heard.

The philanthropists were clever and skillful enough not to take Socrates' old story too literally: that it was possible, simply by asking clever questions, to get everything out of the children. Certain details and explanations had to be given in advance. They were the material which was then "catechized," or dealt with according to the so-called "Socratic-catechetical method."

Now let me take a big step in time, to the beginning of this century in Germany—but also elsewhere—to the era of the *Reformpädagogen* (reform pedagogues), who were opposed to almost anything that was connected with the school of their time. Above all they criticized the prevailing teaching method: as they saw it, a rigorous stuffing of the children's minds with useless and superfluous knowledge. From among the great number of didactic inventions that were advertised with enthusiasm, Berthold Otto's (1859–1933) *Gesprächsunterricht* (teaching through conversation) is especially interesting. Let me offer an example from his diary:

> *April 26, 1906.* Again, it had been a straight chain of reasoning without my needing to interfere to give the discussion a different direction. As before, Irmgard started with astronomy: she asked how often Mars came near the moon. However, those children who had come to know Irmgard better, rejected her question: astronomy is Irmgard's favorite topic; she talks about it persistently, so most of her friends have grown tired of it. The same applies to Richard's wartime stories. We then turned to multiplication—I can't remember exactly why—the principles of which weren't at all clear to the new children among us. I went to the blackboard, and wrote down 7+7+7+7+7, asking the older children to keep quiet. After a while Hildegard finally said that 7 was multiplied by 5. This led us to a discussion on the various fields of mathematics. Trigonometry was unanimously judged as difficult. My question regarding the use of trigonometry initiated a conversation on land surveying in general. Since Kurt, the son of a district valuer, had a lot to tell us, we asked him to give us more details in a future lesson. The descriptions that everything in the streets was measured and mapped, even the distance of the trees from each other, resulted in a discussion on trees, a field of which all children had a surprisingly great knowledge. We finished with a conversation on statistics. (Otto, 1907, pp. 9–10)

Instruction of this kind *questions the authority of the teacher* to decide what the pupils have to learn. Otto's children ask what they want to know, they learn what they want to work on and to learn—like our sons and daughters at the dinner table.

I have come to the end of my exhibition of pictures from the history of instruction. What was I aiming at in presenting this exhibition? I want to suggest that instruction and teaching, of the kind that we see almost anywhere between, say, 9 a.m. and 3 p.m., is an achievement. I wanted to display some didactical *inventions* which, admittedly, are not as spectacular as the invention of welding or chemical fertilizer, but are so important that without them, these more spectacular inventions would be unlikely to exist. In contrast to many radical critics of the school in Germany, I believe that a stroll through the school museum also brings to light many significant advances and inventions we deliberately make use of today.

IN WHAT WAY CAN WE LEARN FROM THE HISTORY OF EDUCATION?[34]

We cannot renounce history, because we were born into it, we have been socialized to it, and, as professionals, are part of it—of the school, or more generally, of education in modern society. "Learning from history" only makes sense insofar as it means coming to terms with a *heritage that cannot be renounced*. So let me explain what I mean by that "learning from history" with the help of three pairs of concepts; I will then sum up and conclude this chapter with the notion of *pädagogische* (pedagogical) *Bildung*.

It is Never the Complete History—Selection and Power

We are in a fortunate situation in that the works the classical writers of education left us as their heritage are all available. However, we are not so lucky when it comes to the practice of instruction in schools. We know only very little about teaching practices in the past, and less about the school's educational or political setting. And to learn about the past of the school, we can only draw from a *selection* of material, from fragments, because little has been preserved. This may seem to be a mere technical problem, but it connects to another issue.

Let me put it this way, there were two different and divergent developments in educational practice and in theory in Germany after the Second World War. On the one side—West Germany—there was the heritage of *Reformpädagogik* and the adoption of Anglo-American concepts; and, on the other—East Germany— there were the achievements of the labor movement and of the Soviet tradition, as well as the achievements of the progressive educationalists. Of course, it was not that simple, but the question is, why this selection and not something entirely different? Why the history of the church and not the history of heresy, as it were? The answer is simple: Because the problem of selection from the past has always been a question of *interests and power*.

If, for example—as in the former German Democratic Republic (GDR)— schools were named after Diesterweg, excellent teachers were awarded Diester- weg medals, and if, in the effort to create a nationwide pedagogical identity, Diesterweg became the favorite "object" of research, the underlying interest is to show that the school system has overcome the deprivation of the underprivileged classes, clericalism, and political reaction, that it is, on the other hand, committed to the modern world, to open-mindedness, and to liberty. In other words, Diester- weg's work was highlighted in the GDR to symbolize for our time, for us today, *a ruling tradition* in education. And, in the same way, Comenius, Francke, Base- dow, Otto, not to mention all the other classics of education are symbols of what we think education should be like.

Tua Res Agitur—Acquisition and Commitment

We can read the history of education and of thinking about education—beginning with Socrates and continuing up to today—as a large document outlining what education *really* is. In this document we find the concepts, practical as well as the- oretical, that have guided teachers and educators up to the present day: Comenius, who in his *Orbis Pictus* made available the world as a whole for teaching practice;

Pestalozzi, who worked out the "natural method" Rousseau had postulated as a basis for education; Herder and Humboldt, who made *allgemeine Menschenbildung* (general education) symbolize the curriculum of the humanistic gymnasium; or Diesterweg, who claimed "general education" for the education of elementary teachers in the 1830s. They were people—like you and me—who worked out these concepts in classroom, in the practice of teacher education, in educational politics, and even in political struggles. And at the same time there were people— like you and me—who in the name of "nature" or "life" fought against "culture" or its "spirit"; who made education a servant of political aims; who forced children to sit upright; or who prepared their minds for a holy war.

When I speak of *acquisition* I think of *all this*: We have to incorporate all of it into our understanding of "education," even if it does not fit into our image of the educational world. Or, let me say it with respect to didactics that it is not only those famous methodical inventions such as the scholastic disputation, the catechetic method of Luther and his followers, Otto's *Gesamtunterrricht*, and Kilpatrick's project method that we should be acknowledging. We also have to take into consideration the odd methods all these inventions were meant to replace, including the well-known odd pseudosocratic language game of our days. The common (and commonly) "bad" practice *and* "progressive" innovations, *all* are significant when we think about "education."

Furthermore all of them—saints and heretics, as it were—were people like *you and me*. Acquisition thus means that the history of education and of the classroom is a medium by which everyone of us can develop and critically reflect his or her competence and identity as a teacher or educator. In principle I am able to practice what they did, and I can interpret education as they did—in good terms as well as in bad.

In this sense I speak of our *commitment* in the history of education. When we refer to our classical writers, let us say, to Herbart *and* to the reform pedagogues who saw him as their counterpart, we speak of human beings, and their thinking about and their practice of education. We ourselves are also human beings and as we refer to these people and their achievements we refer to ourselves, and our teaching, as well. Thus, when I look into Diesterweg's seminar and into Otto's classroom I learn something about myself and my possibilities as a teacher or a teacher educator, just as I do when I look into an "ordinary" classroom of that time.

Judgments and Points of View—Examination and Criticism

"Tradition and acquisition"—this does not mean that everything in the past could or should be relevant for us, for the education of today. It is reasonable, and in fact absolutely essential, that one tradition be identified, interpreted, and distinguished as binding. So, none of us will fill the heads of the young with senseless knowledge—as our proverbial 19th century teachers did. We *will not*, for example, produce authoritarian personalities—the explicit aim of Nazi education in Germany.

And it is *not any* tradition we refer to in this regard, but it is the *tradition of the European movement of the Enlightenment*, starting with Socrates for some, with the French Revolution for others.

Thus, when we recollect chapters from the history of education, we tell our stories in terms of "innovation" as opposed to "conservatism," of "freedom" versus "power," and of "humanity" versus "inhumanity." Moreover, as soon as we decide to venture on education, we are, by definition, part of the tradition of the Enlightenment, which is so deeply embedded in "education" in our modern societies, and we try to understand it by seeking help in those educators whom we define as "classical." But no matter whether we let our classical educators talk in stories or narratives or in pictures, or whether we study their works in a scholarly way, it is always work, interpretation, adoption, translation that we do; in other words, a *critical examination in the tradition of the Enlightenment*. At this point, I come back to the question raised at the beginning of this chapter.

Conclusion—*Bildung* by the Means of History

If history, in the shape of our classical figures, actually offered or represented a lesson for us:

- It would be a lesson defined by the *ruling* interpretation of the world, the ruling *Weltbild*;[35]
- Its acquisition would be possible insofar as we are *engaged in* what history of education may teach us;
- We would need to examine the lesson *critically* if it is to be of use for the orientation of our professional practice.

This is what "learning from history" should be about.

But let me again take up the concept of *Bildung* I introduced in Chapter 2. When I bring this idea into my argument, we can say that work with the heritage that our classics—and the heretics!—have left us may aid us in gaining what I would like to call *pädagogische Bildung*, a formation of educators *as educators*. What does this mean? I will pick up again my explication of the concept of *Bildung* and apply it to education. Let me put it once more in the way of the classical syllogism:

> *Premise 1:* In the history of education in a society, it becomes evident what "education" in that society is.
> *Premise 2*: Educators need to undergo a process of professionalization; that is, to acquire professional knowledge, skills, and orientations.
> *Conclusion:* The study of history, the reflective study of our classics and the historical study of the practice of education and instruction can be a medium of professional identity (*pädagogische Bildung*); that is, a medium for the formation of educators as "educators."

What can we learn from the history of education and instruction? Very little, because it does not offer answers to today's questions and problems. Can we learn from history? Yes, we can, insofar as we can form (*bilden*) ourselves as educators or teachers with the help of the work of our ancestors.

5

Content:
Still in Question?

Some 30 years ago, the German educationist Horst Rumpf (1969) stated that although a significant amount of classroom research had been done in Germany, and more in the United States, the *content* of instruction was not being questioned. The issue he raised is still open. What is the "content of instruction?" I will break this large question down into the following simple questions: What opportunities for pedagogical action become accessible for teachers when they perceive "instruction content" as more than just something prescribed in the syllabus that is to be transferred to the heads of the students? What can a particular content signify to the students who deal with it in their lessons and classes?[36]

In the years that have passed since Rumpf published his criticism, no better answers to these questions have been produced than those already available in the tradition of German Didaktik in the early 1970s. Wolfgang Klafki's "Didactic Analysis" (1995, first published in 1958) was such an answer; that is, an instrument for the structuring of subject matter for teaching (see Chapter 6). The "didactic analysis" was meant to guide the practice of lesson planning, where it was, in fact, working successfully despite all criticism. In Didaktik the rule is that, by and large, teaching will run as planned, provided that the planning is right—and that means, provided that content is stylized according to Klafki's or to others' models of lesson preparation. My interest in the aforementioned questions differs somewhat from that of our student teachers or teacher education students. When I look into classrooms, I want to learn something about what is *happening* (and not what should happen) in them.

In this sense I shall outline my own synopsis of answers to the cluster of questions circling around the question, "what is the 'content of instruction'?" before applying those answers to the question of "instruction content." And, finally, I will use an example of a mathematics lesson in grade 6 (12-year-old students) in an attempt to demonstrate how we could approach a definition and analysis of "instruction content."

WHAT IS "CONTENT OF INSTRUCTION"?

Instruction Content in the Everyday Context of Didaktik

Those who work within the Didaktik tradition use the term *Unterrichtsinhalt* to capture the concept of "content of teaching."[37] By "Didaktik tradition" here I mean the whole body of knowledge, describing the structure, sense, and purpose of instruction in schools and how it may be shaped. I am thinking of what we refer to as "models" and "theories" of Didaktik as well as the experience found in the thousands upon thousands of classrooms from which these models and theories have been distilled.

Through all the theories of Didaktik, we are presented with three core components and their interlocking relationships.

- First, there is the *child*, the youth as student, or rather the Me, the individual, the human self. Proceeding from particular individuals, the Didaktik tradition abstracts, although without denying that the resulting abstract entity represents real young people. Indeed, it sometimes indicates attendant life worlds, relationships, everyday life.
- However, the abstraction is necessary because of the close association with the second component, *reality*, the world, or rather a natural and human world, in the form of knowledge, thus something objective, general, and universal.
- In schools and instruction, both sides are linked by the third component, the *teacher* and the teacher's methodical arrangements.

There are many metaphors for those activities that help to bring together the general and the individual, the objective and the subjective, among them, "reciprocating," "exchanging," "unifying," or "encountering." The often-used term "mediation" recalls philosophical discussion as well as everyday notions of the connection of the general and the individual. The general, the objective side, is perceived as factual, as independently valid; the individual, the subjective side, is perceived as spontaneous as it acquires an understanding of reality. It is these two factors that enable the teacher to function as a link. Sometimes the image of the "didactical triangle" (see Figure 3.1) is used to illustrate this relationship: students–subject matter–teacher.

This much is agreed, regardless of the individual philosophies that the many different parties of German didacticians prefer or simply accept although much is made of discussing the concepts and their meanings in exhaustive detail.

As a rule it is presumed, or in some theories argued explicitly, that the concept of "content of teaching" extends to the out-of-school relationship between students and reality. On the one hand, the objectifications processed in instruction refer to reality, to the world in which we live, to societal practice. On the other hand, students have their own everyday lives outside school, their present and their future lives, their life worlds, which are all a part of societal practice. In this, both sides are connected: the students' work in the classroom on the one hand and their lives on society on the other. Thus, in Didaktik, reflection runs along the following syllogism:

Students work in classrooms.
The objects worked on refer to reality.
Thus, a linkage is provided between students and reality by work in classroom.

In other words, the logic of subject matter is referenced back to societal practice and, by this move, linked to the students' right to cope with their lives in society.

This summary of what I have termed the tradition of Didaktik is intended as an introduction to my argument and, at the same time, as an indication that the concept of "instruction content" refers to a complex nexus of relations, and can only be adequately explained if these relations are made clear. Moreover, the concept also contains a historical dimension. A historically defined form of societal practice is preserved within the "instruction contents." The school "subjects," for instance, which I will discuss later, reflect in their particular arrangement and divisions a body of knowledge about societal practice selected in certain historical constellations. The nexus of complex relations for which the term "instruction content" stands has continued to undergo fundamental and revolutionary change. Though these developments are quite informative, I will skip history here. But, before approaching the complexities I have foreshadowed, let me offer some definitions.

Definitions of Terms

For everyday purposes, the term "instructional content," or "teaching content," is perfectly adequate, but for theorizing and reflecting, particularly under a critical lens, integrative components may be forgotten if there is no appropriate terminology. Reflection is then bound within the very framework (that is, the everyday practice of instruction), that it seeks to address from a distance, from within a critical perspective. Unfortunately, we do not have a consistent set of terms, but the terms themselves are less important than the concepts they define, and with regard to what concerns the concepts, we do have a wide consensus.

Classroom here means *the teaching-learning-working setting as a whole;* the classroom is much more than what educational psychologists describe as the "teaching-learning process." I prefer to describe this process as everything that happens between, say, 10 and 10:45 a.m. within the four walls of a classroom and I shall use the term "classroom" in the following discussion in that way.

Subject or *learning area* are the terms for components of school work defined according to disciplines or fields of practice.

Topic defines a more or less delineated unit within subjects, or an interdisciplinary unit prescribed by the curriculum Thus, we refer to the "topic" of a lesson, of a series of lessons, or of a course.

For everything that is put into words, into pictures, or any other medium—either related to the "topic" or not—I shall use the term *content of the classroom*, analogous to the "contents" of a pocket or a handbag in everyday speech. One subdivision of this content is the contents that are oriented according to, provoked by, and produced in relation to the "topic."

To refer to everything that is produced or collated and recorded as being valid under the guidance of the "topic" in question in the course of instruction, I will use the term *outcome of classroom work*. Such outcomes refer to everything the students are to have at their disposal later on. This concept of "outcome" requires a more detailed explanation.

Ever since the problem of instruction has existed, those responsible for passing on a society's culture have been at pains not only to perform this task (that is, to teach), but also to reassure themselves about the success of their endeavors. The dominant contemporary variant of this concern is found in what Germans call the "objective-orientation": At the end of instruction, students are to have at their disposal, in their heads, hearts, and hands, certain (cognitive, affective, and psychomotor) guides for their lives that are deemed to be correct by those responsible for instruction. But, in that it is impossible to look inside the students' minds, behavior is taken as a pointer. In a way I am going to do just that: I suggest taking the "outcome of classroom work" as an indication of learning processes. In the classroom as a pedagogical situation, as an independent social reality, work results are produced: that is, binding meanings, solutions to problems, or whatever one wishes to call the products. It is these results of the work produced in classroom, though not what occurs in the minds of the students, that I term the *outcomes of classroom work*. The outcome of *learning* is only brought into play in evaluation procedures *after* classroom work has its outcomes.

So, the "content of classroom" reflects the *work* done in classrooms, including the byproducts and the rejects, as well as everything that happens but that does not belong to the "topic" in the strict sense of the word. The product demands validity; that is, it has to be appropriate to the culture that is transmitted in classrooms.

Meyer's henhouses, the translation of a piece of French prose, the faithful rendition of a Bach fugue, or the solution of an arithmetical problem—all demand validity as the product and the knowledge contained within can and should be a guide for the student at the end of a lesson, and beyond.

But let me continue with the definitions. The "subjects" and "topics" of the classroom refer to limited sections of reality outside school, to the practice of people who live and work in society. "Road-safety education," for example, refers to traffic; "environmental education," to changes in the natural world brought about by human intervention and exploitation; "mathematics," to figures and calculations as a means of mastering structures and processes. This human societal practice is present in classroom *in symbolic form* within the "subjects" and "topics": in the wording of science and myths, in the work of art and technology, and so on. *Thus classroom work can be seen as the processing of symbolic representations of societal practice.* And what can be done with symbols? We interpret them. "Work" in classroom means *interpretation*: In the course of classroom work, symbolically coded references to societal practice are "interpreted," as this term is understood in hermeneutics.

"Interpretation" of classroom work not only encompasses the dominant form of text interpretation. The models of poultry farming, for example, that I refer to in Chapter 8 (see Figure 8.1) are an interpretation of the environments in which hens. Hilbert Meyer reports that story in order to further the idea of hands-on learning. Unwittingly, he demonstrates two different *interpretations* of "poultry farming" as well.

The whole body of knowledge that is represented by Didaktik can be slotted into this terminology—from curriculum theory (*Lehrplantheorie*) to subject matter didactics, didactic analysis, and data on the life world of the children. And the framework for this terminology is relatively narrow. It corresponds, metaphorically, to the classroom in the school building, but it does not yet define what makes up the "content of classroom." To come to terms with this concept, *we must consider how the classroom work is related to the environment of classroom.* In the following discussion, I shall confine myself to the topic-oriented content and not explore the byproducts, although these often dominate the entire work.

Production, Selection, and Administration of Knowledge

The "topics" of the classroom are not in a straightforward way related to social practice. They are negotiated by interest groups in society, selected from the universe of knowledge at society's disposal, and stylized and combined to allow them to be used as classroom material. Interest in the success of education is not the only influence at work in this selection and stylization, but coexists with a desire for the reproduction of social conditions as a whole, and for the reproduction of interest groups. Under the title "educational politics" or "the political economy of the educational system," we find explored what Erich Weniger (see Chapter 3) described in his theory of curriculum (*Lehrplantheorie*) as a "struggle to achieve a balance of forces in school and organized learning which corresponds to the relative positions of power held by the factors participating in school." Pierre Bourdieu and Jean-Claude Passeron's (1973) "theory of symbolic power" is an attempt to comprehend the specific function of school and school-based knowledge in the process of social reproduction: the relative prevalence of meaning-bearing topics taught in the school accords with the balance of power. The "universe of knowledge" offered in the curriculum is a problematic, synoptic label for a multiplicity of bodies of knowledge produced in quite different contexts: in everyday life, in trade and industry, in factories, and of course in the sciences. The whole of this knowledge encapsulates human opportunities, both constructive and destructive. It preserves what makes humans human, that is, humane as well as inhumane. In other words, knowledge refers to societal practice in all its variety and historicity or, to put in another way, the "topics" of classroom work reflect societal practice in its fullness and historical determination.

Knowledge, the precipitation of societal practice and human experience, continues to be collected, systematized, handed down, and administered, and science and scholarship are the authorities charged with this task. But science and scholarship do not stand alone in their work on these tasks: *Every* grouping in society—associations, churches, families—collects and administers knowledge, which naturally means that selection is made according to specific interests. An example might illustrate the point:

> Instruction dealing with any of the topics in General Studies at the primary level refers, for instance, to the life of people in their native region, to, as it were, the social production of a focus of local patriotism. At the same time, the topic refers to those who produce the relevant knowledge: local cultural associations, the preservation of local flora and fauna, local history, expatriate organizations, local press, and so forth.

Vague comprehension of such relationships has repeatedly led various educationists to question the ideological overlays of "school knowledge." The call has been for all the mechanisms of selection and tradition to be revealed in order to penetrate beyond school knowledge and grasp unadulterated societal practice. Such expectations are, however, themselves ideologies borne of restricted pedagogical approaches—and of their perpetrators' overestimation of their own capabilities. Reality, call it societal practice or anything else, does not exist in unadulterated form. It exists only in mediated form. Educationists do not need to lament this fact because no one would be able to change it anyway.

I come to an opposite conclusion: The concept of "content of classroom" must be made wide enough to encompass the processes of mediation indicated here. Thus, before knowledge reaches school, it has gone through a multilayered process of production, tradition, and selection. *Classroom work can only be compre-*

hended appropriately if both the knowledge used to create it and the conditions of its genesis are analyzed.

Classroom and World Images

Teaching should take into consideration students' experiences. This maxim encompasses the age-old rule of teaching that says that acknowledging students' experience is the way to improve motivation and learning. At the same time, the maxim expresses the expectation that school teaching must enable students to cope with their lives in the present and in the future. It is an attempt to re-relate classroom work to societal practice.

In the late 1960s, German educationists, for example, Robinsohn (see Chapter 3), imported the forms of discussion of the curriculum that were being used in the United States. They hoped that by providing knowledge of the circumstances and situations of students' future lives, they could derive appropriate forms of educational qualifications that would enable them to deal with these circumstances and situations, which in turn would indicate appropriate contents for the education of young people. But this proved to be theoretically impossible—because future life-situations can, at best, be no more than roughly discerned and classified. And a more definite classification is, pedagogically, undesirable, because it would mean restricting students to particular situations, or classes of situations. The conception of the link between the students' life-world and societal practice cannot be understood as one in which the students' current everyday life, identified as one with societal practice, provides the sole framework for the topics to be covered in classroom. The connection must be interpreted in wider terms.

People living and working in society determine their own particular position, or are placed in a particular position in society. Classroom work guided by the "topic" in question thus refers to societal practice as *the framework given to the students by the scope for self-determination and the fact of (external) determination.* In other words, through classroom work students are to be enabled to acquire for themselves opportunities that humankind has tapped in the course of history, to enhance themselves as human beings, to form (*bilden*) themselves, as Didaktik would traditionally say. In this sense the "outcome of classroom work" may be understood as pieces of an image of the world (*Weltbild*) which students can acquire, as pieces of a framework within which they can take their bearings in their world, a framework that is wider in principle than that which their current and any predictable future life situation would offer.

We need to add something to the Didaktik tradition here. As a rule, Didaktik tends to regard only positive human achievements as being worthy of coverage in classroom. This is based on a selection following the interests of particular groups. Here I am using "achievement" neutrally and universally; the world in which the students must find their own place is also characterized by inhumanity. Both humanity and inhumanity are human.

The Constitutive Rules—Discipline

The "topic" is initially nothing more than a heading, the only delineation being given by the "subject." The classroom work then fills the "topic" with "content," with everything that is put into words or otherwise occurring during the coverage of the topic. Finally, the topic, and the work, is ticked off and logged as a complete and valid "outcome of classroom work." As we have seen, a clear distinction must be made between this and the "learning outcome;" that is, whatever has been formed in the minds of the participants that can be recalled and assessed.

Looked at in all of its details, classroom work follows rules which are, in turn, constitutive of the content. Following Basil Bernstein (1975), we can subsume these rules under the *concept of "discipline."* (The "discipline" of everyday "problems of discipline" is only a small part of the whole.) The following observations may contribute to an explanation, though with no pretence to completeness:

- The "topics" are sorted and thematically classified according to "subjects" or "disciplines."
- They are dealt with in a disciplined manner, in a course vested with authority.
- They are covered outside the context of the participants' daily lives, and in a specific situation that—where necessary—must be maintained in the face of disruption.
- Everyday experiences voiced during the classroom are only included, if at all, to the extent to which they can be, as it were, thematically channeled to fit the course.
- To facilitate the work, societal practice is transformed into a school world.

Since *Reformpädagogik*, Didaktik has often found fault with this separation of school and classroom from life, criticizing it for the alienation, for the loss of meaning to which it can only lead. School critics interpret the disruptions of discipline as an indication of that separation. The rules, however, are not suspended by pedagogically motivated accusations, and there is no reason for them to be suspended. A fixation on particular problems of discipline within schools and classrooms obscures the real problem: the historical achievement that it is the disciplined separation of school from life that makes education possible; that marks out the area in which education can take place; that creates order, however problematic it may be; and that enables young people to interact in pedagogical situations where confusion and disorientation would otherwise threaten. The disruptions of discipline cannot be resolved by the call to abolish discipline, but only by eliminating the causes of disruption.

Within the framework that the previously outlined concepts delineate, scope remains for the further determination of content: determination by the selection from the range of possible "topics"; by the specific method in textbooks and classroom planning; and by the steering of coverage in the classroom by the participants (see Chapter 2 for the "different areas of didactical reasoning"). The example I discuss next follows these instances which determine the content: in the first section, I report on the work itself in a condensed form—a "paraphrase" of the lesson; some explanation of the matter follows; next, I deal with the planning of the lesson; and finally, I refer to the curriculum, that is, to the textbook and to the *Lehrplan*.

"FORTY-EIGHT HALVES CANNOT PLAY BALL"—A MATH LESSON AS AN EXAMPLE

The general reflections set out earlier can be illustrated by an example from mathematics teaching. A case study such as this has the advantage of focusing on a particular lesson and a particular topic, though with the disadvantage that not all aspects touched on can be explored in as much detail as might be wished. But my example should be complete enough to demonstrate the idea.

I shall begin by introducing the lesson. In doing so, I am already moving within the framework marked out by my topic. The headings for each section provide a brief summary of the results of the classroom work, the passages that follow present the individual steps in the work. The social climate of the classroom or the teacher's communication techniques are not in my interest.

{...} is the Set of Divisors of a Number x *from* N^{38}

1. *All possible ways of dividing 24 students into equal squads.* At the beginning of the lesson, the teacher tells the students about "a small problem" in a sports lesson: 24 students are to be divided into squads, with the same number in each squad. The "experts" in the class who know what a squad is first explain the term, then suggestions are made for solving the problem. The teacher picks up "4 groups, with 6 in each" and writes on the blackboard "4 groups, with 6 students in each group," whereupon a student comments "4 times 6." They continue with "8 groups of three," "2 groups and times 12," "6 groups of 4," "24 groups," and "3 groups." The teacher encourages them to think of "all possibilities": "24 groups of one" person "is possible, even though it's something we wouldn't think of in a sports lesson. Still, we'll write it down, because it's conceivable." They continue: "Perhaps 3 groups of 8" and "12 groups of 2." The suggestion "48 groups with a half in each" is rejected, as is "1 group with 3 in each." Finally, "1 group of 24 players" is recorded and with it "all possibilities have been found." The correct answers are on the board in the same format as the first suggestion.

2. *"Task 1".* Working individually the students complete task 1 from their textbooks, which is analogous to the problem they have just dealt with. Beforehand, the teacher had explained the format required for the solution. At the end the results are compared.

3. *The set of divisors of 24 and the definition of "divisor."* The teacher erases "a lot of what we were looking at earlier on in the lesson," but "the most important part remains on the blackboard, namely the number "24," as well as the other numbers, arranged in pairs. "What have all these numbers on the right to do with the one large number on the

left, the 24?" Answers are forthcoming: "You just need to multiply them" and "Add them up or multiply them." The teacher picks up this one: "We could put lots of multiplication signs in here . . . and we always end up with 24." Then the teacher defines that "the numbers 4, 8, 2, 6, 24, 3, 12, 1 . . . are divisors of 24. Divisors of 24 thus are numbers . . . 24 can be divided by."

4. *The notation for divisors of 10 is T(10): = {1,2,5,10}.* Using the divisors of 10 as an example, the correct notation for sets of divisors is presented.

5. *(Homework).*

It should be noted that the time spent on the individual phases of classroom by no means correlates with the length of the sections of my report of the lesson, a point that also shows my emphasis.

The Matter

In order to understand the content of this lesson, the most obvious first step is to examine the relevant discipline, that is, mathematics. From it we gain the following information:

> An integer a (that is, a positive or negative number including zero) is called the divisor of an integer b if there is an integer c and it is true that

$$a * c = b.$$

It can also be said that b is related to a in the relation of "is a divisor of." Therefore, "a is a divisor of b." It follows from the definition that each integer b has the divisors $+1$ and -1, as well as $+b$ and $-b$, termed "trivial" divisors. Numbers that have only trivial divisors are known as "prime numbers." The properties of the divisor relationship are of no further significance for our lesson. It only remains to mention that there are conventions of notation, which have been introduced in the lesson.

In the case of our lesson, only the positive integers are taken into consideration: the divisor relationship is defined in N (that is, in the natural numbers) which is necessary as the students do not yet know negative numbers. Both multiplication ("times") and division ("24 can be divided by") are included into the concept of divisor. The interesting point is the method by which this is done.

Didactical Preparation

We can proceed from a few observations about the lesson itself. First, it can be noted that the divisors of 24, thanks to the practical model (that is, the teacher's "problem" at the beginning), are implicitly given in advance. Other approaches would be feasible. The divisors could be given with the aim of arriving at the divisor relationship by induction. This was the approach taken in the parallel course we observed, but more of that later. It is also noticeable that the relationship is not defined and then used to check divisibility of any numbers. We see by this that the teacher selects one of several conceivable and practicable possibilities.

The "problem" also ensures that discussion is restricted to the natural numbers; that is, the positive *integers*. This is most obviously apparent when a student suggests "48 groups with a half in each." In this case the teacher can point out that they could hardly play with halved students. On the other hand, this approach does involve the difficulty that the trivial divisors can only be managed with some stretching of the "problem." After all, "squads" would not generally consist of a single person or the whole class.

The route taken from the "problem" to mathematics is also striking. It is pointed out that "the most important thing" remains. As this refers to the numbers, it would appear to devaluate the problem. I feel that one can conclude from this step on the teacher's part that the "problem" is not a problem, but serves a purpose external to itself: the restriction to N and the design of the divisors. And, as the teacher says in an interview after the lesson, it also serves to motivate, to commit students to the work set before them. In short, the "problem" serves to *discipline* in the widest sense of the term.

Finally, it is conspicuous that although the route taken to arrive at divisors proceeds—as in mathematics—via multiplication, it is then defined using division ("numbers 24 can be divided by") and without any remainder.

All this has in fact nothing to do with mathematics as such. On the contrary, the simple mathematical facts, the definition of divisors, are restricted, concealed, then discovered, and finally shifted. If we want to find out why, neither mathematics nor the teacher's method will help us much further. If we wish to understand what it is that we are observing, we must examine the context.

The Context

The *textbook* begins in almost exactly the same way as the teacher: "There are 20 students in a class. The sports teacher wants to form squads of equal numbers. What are the possibilities?" The four nontrivial solutions follow, then the question, "Can the teacher also form squads with 6 students in each? This is obviously impossible . . . But the teacher could put all 20 students into one squad or leave each student to compete alone."

There are, however, a few differences from the treatment in the lesson. The book avoids the difficulties with the trivial divisors. The divisor relation is consistently defined through multiplication:

> If the 20 students are divided into 4 squads . . ., there are 5 students in each squad, because $5 * 4 = 20$. The two factors 5 and 4 are termed divisors of 20.

"Multiples" are thus given by "complementary" definition (as defined in the additional material in the textbook). In our example, on the other hand, "multiples" do not come until much later.

The relevant guidelines in the state curriculum, the *Lehrplan*, indicate the topic. Thus, the instruction in this lesson and the textbook are compatible with the guidelines, a point that is almost banal. But the guidelines do yield important additional information as they discuss the organization of grades 5 and 6 where our lesson took place:

> In grade 6 the courses differ with respect to the standard of required achievement and the scope of the content, as well as with respect to the teaching methods. Whereas courses with lower achievement requirements focus on the mastering of arithmetical procedures and the development of strategies for solving concrete problems, the courses with higher achievement requirements progressively address the fundamentals of mathematics.

The students we are dealing with in our example belong to a course "with lower achievement requirements." On the basis of their previous performance, they have been placed in a "C" set for mathematics (in a system of sets A and C) and teaching is to be appropriate to this set. Let us now turn to the teacher, who said in the interview:

> . . . whereas the others [meaning the students in the C-set] have experienced practically nothing but failure in mathematics and can really, I believe, only be motivated if they are looking at something fairly entertaining, . . . something they can grasp, like forming squads in a sports lesson . . . .

And:

> Especially if the subject is rather abstract, not clearly structured, if reassurance such as "right," "good," "carry on like that" is not often forthcoming, the students make no progress at all.

Here we can see that the students are defined, just as the classroom situation, the interpretation of the topic, the work done on it, and its result are themselves determined in advance. The definition moves in what could be described as a practical circle: Students with low academic achievement need concrete instruction (that is, they are not to be taught real mathematics), and the conclusion drawn here for the next step is "bad students." A number of observations become easier to understand when seen in this context, dominated as it is by school organization and guidelines.

We can underline these observations by comparing this lesson with a parallel lesson given by the same teacher in the parallel A-set in the same grade. Here, too, the teacher begins with a mathematics-related situation. But it is more abstract, more removed from reality.

> He reports he has found a jumbled assortment of numbers. He knows nothing about them apart from the fact that they come from two columns of a table. The task is to

find out how these numbers could be ordered. The numbers are, as we soon discover, the divisors of 35 and 48. The students' suggestions include—as was to be expected—ordering the numbers in divisor groups. The teacher picks up this suggestion and asks about the principle of this ordering.

The different approaches the teacher takes in the presentation of the mathematical facts is nicely illustrated when students move outside N. In both of the lessons one of the students happened to allude to the concept of the "fraction,"[39] a fortunate occurrence for the analyst!

> In the C-set John cries, to the delight of the whole class, "48 groups with a half in each." The teacher counters, "Well fine, but how can we split ourselves up into halves?" Gleefully the class volunteers suggestions: "Cut them in half," "You can have half portions, so why not?" The teacher appears to want to follow up these ideas, but John intervenes, "Look, one's pretty fat and one's really thin, so the thin one can be a half." Finally the teacher puts an end to the discussion, "You can't play ball if you are cut in half."

In the A-set George says, "But you can't divide 12 by 24," to which the teacher replies, "Not at the moment, no. Perhaps we'll be able to do it later. But for the time being that's correct."

In the second instance the question of fractions, though not actually discussed, is at least kept open. (In the relevant textbook and guidelines divisors and fractions are explicitly linked.) In the C-set, on the other hand, the discipline of keeping to the so-called concrete example blocks this route, although at least one student creates a simple link with fractions. Moreover, the teacher loses an opportunity to demonstrate a specific achievement of mathematics, which is—in simplified terms—its very capacity to reason in mathematical terms, to operate in detachment from concrete situations. Erasing from the chalkboard also rubs out the links between the concrete situation and the mathematical terms and thus devaluates something of the power of mathematics. Such a restriction only makes sense in connection with the teacher's expectations of the students: They are not expected to be receptive to such achievements.

Now we can understand what I termed the devaluation of the "problem" introduced at the beginning of the lesson. It is less a case of devaluing a practical problem, but more a case of there not being a practical problem at all. What does exist is a student-specific form of mathematics.

Authority and Autonomy

The next question to ask about the content of the lesson given to the C-group would be, *how binding is the orientation given by classroom work in the—mathematical—world?* Behind this question is the problem I have already mentioned of the social groups interested in reproduction and, for that reason, interested in school; the problem of the state as organizing factor in the curriculum, and of the relative autonomy of the education system in society. Here, the focus is, in particular, on the teachers as those in whom the balance of power in society is expressed and who are *at the same* time interested in the students and their future lives. What does all this look like in our lesson?

The topic and the sequence of steps are vested with the authority of the teacher: "There is a small problem I have to tell you about." Behind the teacher's "I" there appears to be, if we can take the teacher's word for it, an anonymous authority the teacher seems to represent and to whom it would seem that the teacher has been instructed to report. The correctness of the outcome of classroom work and the steps taken on the way there are first checked by the teacher. But as a matter of fact validity is not guaranteed by the teacher, nor by that anonymous authority. The validity is guaranteed by the mathematical matter itself, that is, by the logic of mathematics. That is to say that the social interest groups—if there were any—are *hidden behind*, as it were, the processes of selection of content. In this sense we may speak of the "delegated authority" and of the "relative autonomy" of the education system which is analyzed generally in German curriculum theory. Thus, we can observe in fine detail that there is scope for acting pedagogically, however restricted it may be.

The next question is, how much scope for an individual organization of classroom work remains within the limits of higher authorities—be it mathematics or whatever? To state it simply, very little in our case. At no point do our math classrooms open up a perspective outside its immediate confines, neither with regard to subsequent lessons and their topics (as at least the textbook and guidelines do), nor with regard to mathematical relations—not to mention mathematization and the social production of mathematics. But it is not the restriction to the classroom as such that raises pedagogical problems. As I have argued earlier concerning "discipline," one of the achievements of classroom work in school is that it restricts and thus makes ordering and orientation possible. In our case, the problem is rather that the achievement is not recognizable as being an achievement, and that the knowledge worked out in the lesson is not confirmed as an achievement in its own right.

It would be a mistake to make the teacher personally responsible for these limitations as one might do from a strict pedagogical point of view. On the contrary, we can see that, in this case, the teacher was working in ways that are consistent with the educational policy of the region he worked in and with the logic of the subject, (that is, mathematics), in spite of individual variance. Why then, if there seems to be no reason to worry about the teacher's actions and if everything is readily "understandable," am I creating such a complex analysis of what is in practice a matter of course, namely "content"? This question brings me back to the question of the interest that guides such analyses.

CONCLUSION

The concept of "content" in everyday didactics, in the staffroom, and in the teacher training seminar dissolve into a web of relations. These can only be described by reconstructing them individually, an exercise that is always steered by interest. As I have said with express reference to the tradition of Didaktik, educationists are concerned with the *success of education*, that is, the student's *Bildung*. As I explained in Chapter 2, *Bildung* means participation in human tradition or in the tradition of humanity. That means that when analyzing subject matter and content of classroom *Bildung* or an equivalent standard must be incorporated into the concept of "content of classroom" in order to confer sense upon the classroom work. Classroom instruction would otherwise be understood as a mere social technique oriented to educational objectives and not as a pedagogical situation.

Any educationist who fails to pursue the multiple references made by "content" to its preconditions does not grasp this content in its specific quality as a medium for the *Bildung* of students. For such an educationalist, content is nothing but the sum of those pieces of knowledge that have been declared valid. This applies equally to those educationists developing curricula or courses and the like, and to those analyzing the classroom. Any teacher, too, who does not continually strive to pick up the references made by the "topic" has not grasped the latter as the children's own topic and impedes them in the progress of their *Bildung*.

Our parallel math lessons provide a fine example for the *Bildung* argument. In both of the groups, the didactical arrangement restricts the classroom work to N. As I pointed out, this is a pedagogically legitimate restriction. As far as we can judge on the basis of the analysis given in Chapter 2, the teacher opens up the mathematical horizon for the A-group students: "Perhaps we'll be able to do it later." This is a pedagogically legitimate way to deal with the classroom versus real-life disruption. But in the C-group, the horizon remains closed: "You can't play ball if you are cut in half." I evaluate this answer as a hindrance to these student's *Bildung*.

Unfortunately, analyses of lessons like the preceding almost never occur in our teacher education programs. The same can be said of in-service education. As a rule, in both preservice and in-service teacher education, tried and tested scenarios of instruction are passed on; the setting, the methodical arrangement of elements, is the topic. The content is taken as read; it may be questioned from the point of view of its scientific accuracy, but not in any other respect. All this is greatly to the detriment of the teachers and their opportunities for action, that means, their opportunities for a "pedagogical construction of reality in classroom."

6

Didactics As
Construction of Content

In their well-known study on *The Language of the Classroom,* Arno A. Bellack and his collaborators analyzed "the teaching process through an analysis of the linguistic behavior of teachers and students" (Bellack, Kliebard, Hyman, & Smith, 1966, p. 1). They identified "pedagogical moves" and were able to find and describe "teaching cycles." More precisely, they were able to reconstruct certain rules followed by participants in classroom discourse. They looked at classroom instruction as a "language game" and interpreted it accordingly, developing concepts that enabled them to describe and interpret the game as one that indeed follows rules. The object of their study was not the classroom as a whole, but classroom discourse.

In this context they "were also interested in the dimensions of meaning represented by the *content* of the messages communicated" (p. 5), that is, instructional meanings and substantive meanings, although they were not able to come up with much on this score. They identified "*substantive* meanings," which refer to the main concepts of the textbook on which the instruction was based, and "*substantive-logical* meanings," that is, "cognitive processes involved in dealing with the subject matter." However, in the end, they could do no more than count frequencies of the categories and subcategories of their "content." They were astounded at the differences between classrooms in the area of substantive meanings: It was "remarkable," "particularly in relation to the similarities found in the pedagogical area." (pp. 69, 72, 85) In other words, they did not know what to make of their findings.

I can remember quite exactly the questions that came into my mind when I first read *The Language of the Classroom*: Why cannot the findings be readily interpreted? Is "content" of classroom discourse a vague concept and not a clearly defined variable? And if that is the case, what might the concept "content" mean?

TABLE 6.1.   Cutting Tools

Opening (Teacher)	Answering (Pupil)	Follow-up (Teacher)
Now,		
All eyes on me.	NV	
Put your pencils down.	NV	
Fold your arms.	NV	
Hands on your heads.	NV	
Hands on your shoulders.	NV	
Fold your arms.	NV	
Look at me.	NV	
Hands up.	Paper clip.	A paper clip good.
What's that?		A paper clip.
		There we are.
And what's that?	A nail.	A nail well done.
Janet.		A nail.
And hands up.	A nut and bolt.	A nut and bolt good
What's that one?		boy a nut and bolt.
That's got two names a double name.		
…		
And this.	Hacksaw.	A hacksaw yes a
What's this a picture of?		hacksaw.
Abdul.		
Fine,		
And the last picture of all,	An axe.	An axe yes it's an
I've got there what's that?		axe.
Danny.		
…		
Now then,		
I've got some things here, too.	Saw.	It's a saw yes this is a saw.
Hands up.		
What's that what is it?		
What do we do with a saw?	Cut wood.	Yes.
		You're shouting out though.
What do we do with a saw?	Cut wood.	We cut wood.
Marvelette.		

Source: Adapted from Sinclair & Coulthard, 1975, pp. 90–94.

TWO PICTURES BY WAY OF ILLUSTRATION
OF MY QUESTION

Let us examine an example of classroom discourse more closely. I have chosen a detail from a lesson that John M. Sinclair and Malcolm Coulthard report in their book *Towards An Analysis of Discourse* (1975; see Table 6.1).

Our first reaction to what we see in this classroom is probably annoyance at the gruesome drill, but that drill is not my concern here. The framework of the transcript indicates the linguistic angle from which Sinclair and Coulthard comprehend instruction, but an elaboration on the linguistic aspects of the classroom is not my focus either. What I am concerned with is what is dealt with in classroom. But it is not easy to say what the students deal with. Thus, in the lesson:

- There are pictures of things that can cut and be cut.
- The materials are assigned to the respective cutting implements.
- Categorization is commenced, with "materials" as a generic term.
- Objects are identified by their names and by their everyday uses.

Obviously, everything in this lesson is somehow connected with the "content." The matter is complex but at the same time wonderfully transparent:

- We have, for example, a pair of scissors, a *tool,* characterized by its everyday use.
- "Scissors" is also a *name* that we can use to put the object at our disposal ("Give me the scissors").
- And there are the *pictures* of "materials," which present, within a teaching context, the everyday world in which the tools are used and described.

When I thought about this structure, I remembered Johann Amos Comenius and his *Orbis Sensualium Pictus* (originally published in 1658; see Chapters 4 and 9 for more detail). Sinclair and Coulthard are not Comenius. Their approach is pragmatic-linguistic and not didactical. But the lesson they report has exactly the same structure as Comenius's 300-year-old textbook. We see, for example, in Figure 6.1:

- *Pictures* that represent things, "materials"
- The *things* being embedded in an everyday situation in which they are *used* according to the rules of life in society
- *Words* in a meaningful text referring to those things

In other words, we find the very same *logic* in the *Orbis* and in Sinclair and Coulthard's lesson; namely, the didactical logic of the correspondance of tools, their names, and their uses.

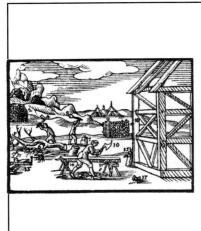

Faber Lignarius	Der Zimmermann
afciat *Afcia* 10	zimert mit v Zimeraxt 10
Materiam,	das Bauholz/
unde cadunt	davon fallen
Affulæ; 11	die Späne; 11
& ferrat *Serra,* 12	un feeget es mit v Seege/12
ubi *Scobs* 13	da die Seegfpäne 13
decidit;	davon ftäuben;
Poft elevat tignum	Darnach legt er dz Zimer
fuper *canterios* 14	auf Böcfe 14
ope *Trochlea,* 15	mit Hülff v Winde/15 (16
affigit *Anfis* 16	befäftet es mit Klaniern/
lineat *Amuffi;* 17	meffet es mit der Richt-
	(fchnur; 17
Tum compaginat	Alsdann paaret er
Parietes 18	die Wände 18
& configit trabes	und füget die Balfen
Clavis trabalibus. 19	mit Zimmernägeln. 19

Source: Comenius, 1978, p. 130.

FIGURE 6.1.   The carpenter.

My looking into Sinclair and Coulthard's classroom (Table 6.1) and at Comenius's picture (Figure 6.1) is intended to highlight the issues I will be exploring in this chapter. What we know is that "content" *exists* in classrooms. Furthermore, "content" has been solidly elaborated in the Didaktik tradition. But what, exactly, is the "content" of classroom instruction? I will try to *conceive*, that is, to understand the logic in it.

THE CONTENT OF CLASSROOM DISCOURSE

First of all, let us return to the concept of *Bildung* that I sketched in Chapter 2. It was Wolfgang Klafki (1995) who, within the framework of *Bildungstheorie*, developed an instrument for the structuring of subject matter for teaching termed *didaktische Analyse* (didactic analysis). More precisely, he asked the question, what is the *Bildungsgehalt,* (that is, the contribution to the pupils' *Bildung*, of a *Bildungsinhalt*, a traditional term within Didaktik that he uses for this analysis and which means an element of the curriculum)? He goes on to subdivide his question into five *more detailed* groups of questions that may be used to examine every topic of instruction (see Chapter 2). The answers to these questions summarize the *Bildungsgehalt*.

There has been a long and fruitful (though, on many occasions, also unfruitful) discussion of Klafki's scheme, but I will not explore that discussion here. I am interested in "content" from an analytical rather than a constructive point of view.

So, let us ask more precisely what the content of classroom work is. In Chapter 7, I will pose this problem with respect to a mathematics class as follows: What does mathematics mean in this case? What do probability, outcome, pairs of numbers, frequency, and so on mean in the context set up by this lesson (and by the lessons that preceded it)? I do not ask for the ideas within the minds of the pupils and I do not intend to look into their heads. I am interested in the knowledge that is worked out and stated as valid in this particular lesson. Here, I will be looking at an art class and testing the concept of "content" I am going to develop.

Symbolic Representation of Reality

First of all, we need to recognize that it is not reality itself that is present in classroom work but rather a symbolic representation of reality. The real objects, scissors, knives, guinea pigs, or international economics, have been removed and transformed into texts and pictures—and brought into the classroom in this form. Here they *refer to* reality, to everyday life, to social practice. In other words, in the classroom the presentation of reality is exclusively coded in the language of one or another symbolic system. But at the same time, all these symbols *are* reality. They are real things within the world of school: A poem is read and does not represent only something else; a nesting box is built, and does not only represent some sort of bioeconomic context.

I have mentioned language and pictures, but that is rather vague. Ernst Cassirer (1956) analyzed different *symbolic forms*: myth, religion, science. We can differentiate further and think in particular of the different symbolic systems of the sciences. In Bellack's experiment, for example, it was the language of economics, and in my example with the two dice, it was mathematics (see Chapter 7).

In the language of didactics we can now say that "subject matter" is encoded in symbolic forms. It is not the practice itself, not reality itself that is dealt with in the classroom, but *the subject matter refers to this reality*. I could just as well speak of "culture" and, incidentally, mention that Theodor W. Adorno (1972) in his famous essay on *"Theorie der Halbbildung"* (smattering of Bildung), defined *Bildung* as "culture insofar as the subject has acquired it" (p. 94). Or, like Georg Wilhelm Friedrich Hegel (1770–1831) and later German philosophers, I could refer to the "objectifications of the spirit": "cultural assets" (*Kulturgüter*), as we often say today. And it was Hegel's concept that lies behind the passage from Marx I quoted in Chapter 2. No matter how we formulate it, the concept of the symbolic representation of reality is appropriate for, on the one hand, understanding precisely what subject matter in the classroom is and, on the other hand, for finding the link to the concept of *Bildung*, the cultivation of humanity in the individual by the acquisition of those attributes in which humanity is objectively manifested.

Lehrplan and Selection

So, we now have culture, but we have not yet reached the classroom. Of course, "humanity," however freely accessible, is not something that is at the disposal of teaching. Heads are too small, books too slim, and time too short. Moreover, there are any number of parties keen on seeing a particular choice made. Apart from the more technical restrictions, there are at least two selection principles—political power and pedagogical authority:

- By means of political power, those cultural assets are selected that represent the dominant culture.
- By means of pedagogical authority, a selection is made in the interests of society's young.

Here we are at the center of what we in German would call the *Lehrplan*, which is usually but not quite adequately translated as "curriculum." In *Lehrplan theory* these processes of selection are elaborated theoretically and researched empirically.[40]

Before I now plunge into teaching, first a reminder: The subject matter that enters the classroom as the representation of humanity, that is, of what makes human beings human (see Chapter 2), has already been selected for the classroom—in the final instance by the teacher who in one person must represent the interests of both the dominant culture and the pupils.[41] But this subject matter is not only selected, it is *shaped* in a specific way, for a didactical purpose. The school curriculum is not something like a reduced copy of the corresponding academic discipline; instead, it is framed and composed according to a specific didactical logic.

Acquiring Humanity: Work in the Classroom

The mere presence of cultural assets does not suffice for learning—at least not in our society—even when these cultural assets have been selected under pedagogical considerations. What happens, then, with the subject matter in the classroom?

For Bellack and his collaborators, international economics was the object of a "discourse." There were particular "cognitive processes involved in dealing with the subject matter" (Bellack, Kliebard, Hyman, & Smith, 1966, p. 5); that is, in their view, analytical, empirical, and evaluative processes. But there are other "processes" we can observe: throwing two dice, solving a system of equations, singing a song, or knitting a sock. We need a concept that describes more precisely than "deal with" what happens during instruction. In the German Didaktik tradition we use the term *Arbeit* (work).

Today, we read a lot about *Handlung*, action, hands-on activity, which probably means the same as *Arbeit* or work, as used in *Reformpädagogik*. In the wake of

Soviet "activity theory" the concept of "learning activity" was elaborated and introduced into the discussion, though not in the mainstream, of Didaktik. Neither concept is satisfactory. The first usually contains little more than the demand that the pupils should do something using their hands (as the German word **Handlung** would seem to suggest), while the latter might be restricted to reconstructing internal psychic processes in psychological terms, and then localizing these in the "pedagogical process," as it is termed. In other words, it is a form of "psychodidactics," important enough, granted, but it remains unclear how this concept is linked with the classroom as a *pedagogical* institution.

I would suggest conceptualizing work in the classroom as *interpretation*. If we try to understand what pupils and teachers do during instruction under the term of *work* (that is, as a medium for human becoming human), what do we see? If we understand the object of work as symbolically coded cultural assets, as I have done, then the work can be fittingly conceived of as *interpretation* of these objects. What else can we do with *symbolic* coded reality?[42]

Two things are particularly important in connection with the concept of "interpretation" as I am using it in this context. First, we need to pinpoint the specific characteristics of the object being dealt with in instruction; that is, of the symbolically coded reality. In other words, one can speak of *the didactical construction of reality*.[43] And, second, this concept allows individual actions to be interrelated meaningfully in teaching, as in the concept of teaching cycles, which, as we know, enables pedagogical moves to be comprehended as sequentially meaningful. "Soliciting" and "reacting," or "question" and "answer" are not to be seen as they are in everyday communication. We rather have to see them as steps on the way— at the end of which we find both the *product,* that is, the map drawn in the students' textbooks to which the question directs them, and the *Bildung* of the producer, that is, the map in the students' minds. And "praise" or "reproach" are to be understood as means for sustaining this pedagogical process. From this viewpoint it does not make much sense to count one or another kind of pedagogical move, and then interpret their frequencies. If we want to understand the content of classroom work—its structure and development—we have to reconstruct the full set of complex processes that are found in every classroom and every lesson.[44]

The Pedagogical Legitimation of Work in Classroom

Classroom work in school—whether it is conceptualized as "interpretation" or anything else—differs in one essential characteristic from productive work in society. Hilbert Meyer (1980), a leading advocate of the orientation of teaching to the principle of action, *Handlung*, writes:

> In hands-on-learning, teachers and pupils together try to do something with their heads, their hearts, their hands, their feet, and with all their senses. This can lead to

results which are of meaningful utility for teachers and pupils. (p. 211, my translation)

What he is forgetting here is that a classroom is—a classroom. It is good, even indispensable, that the products of work in the classroom have a meaning, a use for the children. But where exactly does this use lie? Susanna's mother, or indeed Susanna's elder brother, can embroider the tray cloths much more quickly and expertly than Susanna; nesting boxes are much cheaper in the supermarket; the "*Hallelujah Chorus,*" with the whole *Messiah* thrown in, is performed much better by a professional choir than by the school orchestra with Alexander playing solo. And yet we are pleased with the tray cloths; we hang up the slightly crooked nesting box; and we go along to the school's Christmas recital, although we really do not have the time. Why? Surely not because of the utility value of these things. No, we go because the products are *signs* that our children have acquired something and, at the same time, have made something out of themselves. Crooked and off-key they may be, but we are prepared to accept what we would never accept from a carpenter or a virtuoso, as long as we can be sure that the children have worked as though the future of the world depended on it, in other words, seriously and with dedication. And, as a matter of fact, their future does depend on it.

Such work is embedded in a pedagogical situation, in teaching. In this way its product is the proof-of-the-pudding situation and the pedagogical purpose with which the situation is organized. A utilitarian object for us, or for the children, can be motivating and is sometimes needed to maintain the situation, but it is not the essence of a *pedagogical* situation. On the contrary, talking about "usefulness" and "application" only obscures the real contents and the real pedagogical purpose that legitimizes classroom work.

These reflections about the pedagogical construction of reality in school must be followed by the question, what is this pedagogically constructed reality actually like? So, research on teaching has to analyze the content generated in the pedagogically legitimated language game of instruction. The question is, what image of the world is produced in the work done in the classroom; that is, what is the image we expect the pupils to adopt as their own? Let me now give an example.[45]

MANUELA AND THE BRICK: APPLYING THE CONCEPT TO AN ART LESSON

An Everyday Course in Art

The subject is art, an elective subject in the 10th grade of a German Gymnasium, taught for two lessons a week as an alternative to music. The topic given by the

Lehrplan is "Space—Form and Function," and as possible contents of lessons it suggests "town planning, housing conditions, construction methods, and so on". In these fields the students are required to develop "vivid ideas, an observant mind and ways of representation."

For several weeks this class has studied historical and modern architectural designs and ground plans. The teacher, in his early thirties, had originally intended to continue along this line until the end of the school year (there are two months left). However, the pupils (12 girls, 5 boys) had asked for practical lessons and had chosen pen-and-ink drawing within the frame of the overall topic "architecture." The teacher prepares his lessons accordingly, beginning with revision and exercises. In this context:

> . . . the third phase [of the course] is intended to be productive; here, the emphasis lies on acquiring skills and techniques needed for the creative assignment as well as sketching and drawing a facade.

We videotaped three lessons. During the lessons preceding our first recording, the pupils had had time to become familiar again with drawing with pen and ink and to remember the possibilities and opportunities that this medium offers. This activity was followed by a task aimed at improving the students' skills: A brick had to be examined and drawn, paying attention to perspective and the brick's specific surface structure, without using outlines as technique.

In the first lesson we recorded (let us call it the "brick lesson"), this assignment was completed and its results were being "discussed" and "analyzed." At the end of the lesson, the teacher announced that "perhaps we'll talk about one or two aspects again tomorrow, and then we will try the whole business again on a larger scale."

At the beginning of the following lesson, the second one we recorded, the teacher sums up:

> Yesterday we talked about the work with the bricks, and I think we pointed out criteria for the realization of the surface structure of a body. We also discussed why some techniques had better be avoided, for instance drawing outlines . . . and when to use different kinds of hatching.

He then set a new task, the creative assignment that the preceding exercises were intended to prepare the class for. However, this task was not the originally planned representation of a facade, as the teacher told us:

> As a result of the difficulties that arose in connection with the pen-and-ink drawing, I dropped the idea of the facade . . ., because it would have been too time-consuming. . . . but a still life: to bring together different materials in one picture and to restrict the pupils to objects they all have access to, as there are stones, sponge, pieces of wood, etc.

With the help of a transparency the teacher tells the students how to arrange the various objects because the rules for the composition of a still life had not been discussed. "In order to get at least some results I thought I'd better tell them how to arrange their objects." This means that the pupils' artistic freedom is limited to the choice of shape and surface structure of the single elements of the still life. "You are free to choose any object you like. It does not matter what you take. However, the objects should be arranged in the same way as on the transparency." After further explanations the pupils start working. They have four periods to complete their task. In contrast to the sketches of the brick, these pictures will be graded and entered into the students' evaluation.

No German teacher, and no art teacher in particular, will have difficulties understanding the lessons described. They represent everyday instruction of the kind that can be found at any school. But let us have a closer look.

The Underlying Pattern: Techniques—Effect

At the end of the "brick lesson" the students discussed and compared their drawings. The teacher asked them:

> . . . to have a close look at each picture. Please, ask yourselves: Which pictures look like a stone? which do not? and why? Let's then try to put down some rules: which techniques had better be avoided and which should be preferred in order to achieve the effect of a stone?

Techniques on the one hand and their effect on the other: This is the underlying pattern of all of the lessons we observed. In the "brick lesson" the techniques were dots, lines, and their combinations and variations; the effect was the effect of a stone. (Let us observe that the teacher only talked about the "stone," not the "brick.")

The pattern "techniques-effect" can be found in the teacher's instructions to the "brick lesson" as well as in the discussion of the drawings:

> *T.:*   Yes, well, how should the hatching be performed if the picture is to resemble a stone?
>
> *Pupil 1:* I think these lines are a bit too straight.
>
> *T.:*   Em, look here, for instance, this bit where all lines go into one direction. I think we have to ask ourselves whether straight lines are at all suitable for drawing a stone.
>
> *Pupil 2:* I think they aren't, because there aren't any straight lines in a stone.

We also find the pattern in one of the rules for the composition of the still life. The teacher dictated:

> Form and surface structure are to be varied to the effect that (a) the contrast between circle and rectangle is maintained and that (b) the bodies are as different as possible.

And while explaining the task, he said to Petra:

> It should be a plastic motif with a certain surface quality. You know, it doesn't matter whether you choose an imaginative or a real motif; it might even look funny if you said I'd like to draw a coffee cup with the surface structure of, let's say, a brick or a bearskin.

And a bit later:

> . . . one requirement is that the motif you choose possesses a certain surface structure that must be conveyed in the drawing. It should be drawn so graphically that you would want to touch it.

It is not difficult to identify this pattern of techniques and effect. Whenever the assignment was the subject of discussion in class, it became apparent. And our recordings show that it was in fact the underlying pattern of the whole unit, whether in the teacher's working instructions and the students' realizations or the discussion of the results.

Does this mean that we have understood the lessons only because we identified their underlying pattern? Most unlikely. Hardly anybody would view a series of lessons without requesting further particulars and explanations. Neither did we. We asked the teacher, "Why did you do this or that?" because we did not understand all our observations or all the teacher's decisions.

An Unexpected Problem

Let us describe two episodes that may illustrate such a problem:

1. At the beginning of the "still-life lesson," Beate asked, "Couldn't I just start drawing some kind of a structure and then say, well, this looks like wood, so it is wood? I mean, without having intended it?" The teacher answered:

> Well, let's put it this way, people who didn't know what your motif was or what you had in mind must be able to gather from your picture: this is a piece of wood, a stone, cardboard or whatever.

The piece of wood, the stone, the cardboard or any other object the teacher might bring along does not have to be examined; the pupils simply draw away, and if their drawings resemble wood, well, then they are right! Although the teacher assumes that Beate had an object in mind which could then be "gathered" (which in fact she did not!), his answer supports her view all the same, as does his answer to Petra's question, "It doesn't matter whether you choose an imaginative or a real motif" (see earlier passage).

2.   In the "brick lesson," the camera was focussed on Beate and Manuela; they were sitting next to each other and Beate was drawing without regarding the brick lying in front of her. She was hatching and dotting. Manuela, on the contrary, looked up every now and then and took the stone into her hands to examine it from every perspective.

> *B.:*   You didn't bring your copy of the Schiller, did you, or else I could've finished reading it.
> *M.:*   Why, are you done with your drawing?
> *B.:*   Mh (affirmative), finished it last night.
> M.:   Without a model?
> *B.:*   Yes! (Manuela taps her forehead.)
> *M.:*   You're crazy!
> *B.:*   (laughing) I am, aren't I?

Manuela continued drawing quickly. She looked up again and again, attentively studying the stone lying in front of her, while Beate, with her back to the stone, was working on her second drawing. From time to time Manuela compared her drawing with Beate's first one and the stone.
Some time later the teacher announced:

It's now 10:50, and I'd suggest that you stop drawing at 10 past; that'll give us time to discuss at least some of the works. I don't want to spend too much time on this exercise.

Manuela's hands started moving more and more quickly. She was drawing lines across the whole sketch and hardly regarded the brick any more. Beate remained perfectly calm, watching Manuela with a smile.

> *M.:*   Beate, please, have a look. What do you think, doesn't it look more like a stone now?
> *B.:*   Reminds me more of an aquarium.

After a while Manuela remarked:

> *M.:*   I've never drawn a stone as quickly as today!
> *B.:*   In fact, you've never drawn a stone at all.

Beate takes a closer look at Manuela's drawing:

> *B.:*   Why don't you use your imagination?

Manuela makes a few changes.

> *M.:*   That's better.

From then on Manuela made several corrections, completely ignoring the stone in front of her. The teacher started collecting the drawings and fastened them to the blackboard. Manuela went on hatching intensively for a while—we could even hear the pen scratching across the paper—before she handed her drawing to the teacher.

At first sight, episode 1 seems to be another example of the pattern "techniques-effect of the stone." However, the conversation between Manuela and Beate (episode 2) shows that there is an underlying problem with the content. Each girl interpreted and carried out the assignment differently: Manuela examined the brick closely and attentively, trying to capture even the smallest detail of the model-stone. Again and again she compared her graphic representation of the brick with the original, without growing tired of making corrections. Beate, on the contrary, finished her drawing at home. She has drawn a stone as it existed in her imagination. She did not bother to verify this imagination or, if necessary, correct it.

What kind of abilities does Manuela have to possess if we want to understand her utterances and her artistic performance? It is abilities on a scale from sensual understanding to the methodical use of various techniques. Although her drawing does not reveal these abilities, we can assume that they exist, because we heard what she said and we watched her drawing. Unfortunately, we could not compare Manuela's picture with her model-stone; that might have given us further evidence. For this reason, we refrained from including a copy of her drawing; we would have had to include the stone as well.

Beate's drawing on the other hand may be as "stony" as Manuela's, but there is a difference between both of them. Beate did not take the trouble of studying a model; she knew how to produce "the effect of a stone" and acted accordingly. She possessed the same skills and techniques as Manuela, but, and this is the important difference, she apparently did not comprehend the stone sensually. Nevertheless, both Manuela and Beate solved the assignment—in quite different ways—and their drawings more or less met the expectations of the teacher.

By the way, our episode indicates the difference between the process of working and the product worked out. Supposing that both drawings convey the impression of "stone"; the abilities brought in and worked on in the classroom obviously differ. Beate draws according to an algorithm as it were, while Manuela observes and links her observations with the techniques she has at her disposal.

Can we explain this episode simply by referring to different methods of working or to different character traits? Of course not! The episodes described here clearly show that the teacher has no little part in the development of two different interpretations. At the beginning of the "still life-lesson," he did nothing to correct Beate's understanding of the assignment and, in fact, his remarks even supported her assumption. (Of course, he did not overhear Beate's and Manuela's little discussion.)

To this point, our example demonstrates a specific interpretation of the sequence: brick-facade-architecture. The teacher's emphasis lay in the corresponding method of interpretation; that is, the pen-and-ink technique. The product of the classroom work was a series of drawings. Our excerpts from the classroom discourse make clear that the teacher's pedagogical interest lay in the process of production and the students' acquiring of the technique in question rather than in the product itself.

However, there are a few more aspects that we need to consider. One has already been mentioned: the limited time. It is circumstances like this that we will be looking at and examining now.

The Teacher's Lesson Preparation

Knowledge of what a teacher intended is imperative for the understanding of what a teacher says or does. Our teacher had planned three different steps or phases:

- Revision of and refreshing different techniques
- Exercise ("brick lesson")
- Creative assignment (facade)

Each step was to take its legitimacy from the following one. In order to be able to draw a brick, the students must be reminded of the techniques; in order to be able to put on paper the texture of a facade, they must be familiar with the texture of a brick which is one element of a facade. This means that the surface structure of the facade gave each single step its educational purpose.

Bearing this in mind, the teacher's answers to Beate's question (see episode 1) are understandable. It was neither the one and only model-stone that mattered nor the individual experiences of the students, but the "stony" aspect of a stone, its texture, and the command of techniques that may serve to represent it.

The discussion in class showed, however, that the students were not able to meet the teacher's requirements and the teacher confirmed this impression in the inter-

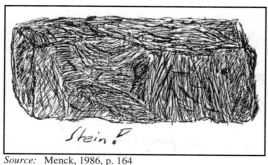

Source: Menck, 1986, p. 164

FIGURE 6.2.   Stone from the art lesson.

view. One pupil was obviously aware of his inability "to get across the effect of a stone." To be on the safe side he wrote "*Stein!*" (stone!) underneath his drawing (see Figure 6.2). Considering these deficiencies, we might have expected that the teacher would give his students additional time to practice their skills, or that he would ask himself whether the medium (pen-and-ink) was appropriate given the time. Instead, what followed was a new assignment, again with the emphasis on "surface structure," and it again required skills that the pupils had not yet acquired.

If we only considered the teacher's lesson preparation, we could say that the teacher made a serious mistake. But it is not that simple; the teacher's preparation was based on a certain concept of art education that has to be taken into consideration as well.

The Teacher's Concept of Art Education

The teacher whose class we have been examining believes that successful instruction requires a sequence of steps planned in advance, in order to attain an intended goal; only a detailed plan and the orientation toward a set goal prevents the learning process from taking an unforeseeable direction. He also believed explicit formal grading should be part of art education; only then could grades in art be compared to those in other subjects. Consequently, he sets tasks and assignments that require specific techniques that can be practiced and developed by all pupils. He also lays down criteria for the final assessment of the students' results, ignoring artistic talent or individual expressive power.

The teacher's ideas about successful art education began to develop during his education in art at the university. On the one hand, his studies followed the tradition of the Bauhaus; on the other hand, he was particularly attracted to surrealism. It looks as if it is this attraction to both of those traditions that is responsible for the essential characteristic in his classes: the development and sophistication of techniques and skills—the pattern of technique and effect, as we called it—and the restriction of the students' artistic freedom, as it can be seen in the teacher's working instructions to the still life.

The teacher told us that his ideas of successful teaching were also substantially influenced by his experiences during his *Referendariat,* that is, the 2 years of internship. These 2 years at a teacher training college and at a German high school shaped and formed his view of a good teacher. He became convinced that consistency of work instruction and of the working process is one of the most important principles a teacher should adhere to: following a strict plan, meeting deadlines and observing rules of social behavior. The teacher spells out his intentions, his rules and expectations accordingly and as a result, he tells us, he does not have to worry about lack of discipline or motivation, and grading the pupils' work becomes easier.

The teacher's didactical concept reveals the nature of the pedagogical legitimation of the lessons we have been looking at from the teacher's point of view. Furthermore, it links the classroom work we have seen with the context that defines the "text"; that is, the content of our lessons and the work in the class. For a more detailed analysis, we would have to go one step further and would have to ask ourselves how far characteristic features of the classroom as an institution can be traced in the analyzed lessons. But that would require a chapter of its own.

CONCLUSION

Our analysis was meant to help us understand what instructional content is really about. But to do this we had to reconstruct the pedagogical construction of reality in a classroom. The topic of our lessons was worked out according to the framing factors and in view of the students' learning process. We interpret this process as their acquiring instruments that they have at their disposal and as their forming of their selves or their *Bildung.* This takes us back to our initial general reflections.

German Didaktik theorists and teachers who might have followed our analysis will not fail to make the—well-known—objection: Look at the real stone in my one hand and at the stony-looking drawing in the other: This is a striking example for the separation of school and the "real world." I have never really understood why they worry. It is just this separation that enables school to make its specific contribution to society, namely *Bildung,* precisely because it is *not* industry, it is *not* work on the production line, at the computer, or in an architect's office. In school the reality of these—and many other—sections of the world is first made manageable by symbolic representation. Drawing with pen and ink within the confines of the classroom *enables* Manuela to *perceive* the specific structure of a brick, which outside the classroom *disappears* in a facade. More generally speaking, the aforementioned disruption is pedagogically legitimate insofar as children are prevented from being crippled or destroyed if they want to acquire a tiny bit of their world, as they were in the 19th century by child labor. Didaktik theorists have always, and quite justifiably, complained that it is often not the world in which we live, or only a small part of it, that our readers, mathematics problems, and chemistry experiments acknowledge and refer to. As long as it is a medieval or even a fictitious world, they are right with their criticism. But we cannot throw out the baby with the bathwater and denigrate the achievements that school and classroom instruction have brought about, and which only they can obtain.

7

Throwing Dice: The Content of a Math Lesson

In this chapter, I return to the phenomenon that I discussed more generally as the "content of classroom" in Chapter 6 and that is generally known in schools as "subject matter." Though there are some fruitful approaches to understanding what subject matter might mean deriving from classroom research[46] and the sociology of knowledge,[47] we are far from understanding what "content" or "subject matter" means *at the classroom level*.

In Chapter 6, I sketched out some ideas on "content," trying to make use of concepts derived from several theoretical perspectives.[48] My concern now is to test these ideas by analyzing another example of classroom work. Any lesson could serve this purpose, but I will discuss a math lesson that I came across in a booklet entitled *Understanding Children Talking*.[49] An advantage of this example is that the lesson took place in a British school (and not a German one). Although there is little information in the booklet on the context and although the full lesson is not presented, it serves my purpose quite well, to explore my approach to "content of classroom."

PARAPHRASE OF THE DOCUMENT

First of all, let me give a brief summary of the content of the lesson. It consists of a title containing the outcome of some classroom work and of a report of the work itself.

> *The outcome of throwing two dice simultaneously.*
> *a. The outcome and different ways of describing it.*
> "Each child was given a pair of dice, and was asked to throw them once." The teacher asks for the outcome. Results such as, "eight" were given as well as "six and two." The teacher leaves open which of them he would prefer, and writes both of them on the board; the two ways of describing the outcome are "saying them separately" [that is, the "six and two" way] and "add them together" [which results in "eight"]. There is not just one right way—so "there are two ways."
> *b. The number of different outcomes with the pairs.*
> Now the teacher asks for the different outcomes from throwing the two dice: "How many . . . do you think there are?" The pupils' answers are: 12, 6, 18, 24, 8. The pupils begin guessing, then the teacher asks for an explanation: "How did you get 24?" Kim explains. The teacher "starts listing the pairs on the board and the children continue this in their books."
>
> Interrupting their work, he asks for new guesses and explanations: 36 is given— the explanation being: six numbers on each dice and two dice at hand. Another pupil suggests 16–6 in the first column of a pair of numbers, fewer in the next (I will come back to these explanations later on). Afterward, the class is to complete the columns. (This part of the lesson is not completely recorded.)
> *c. The meaning of frequency*
> "In a later part" of the lesson the teacher introduces the word "frequency." Several meanings are given: "continuous," the "number of cycles a wave makes," "quite often." The teacher concludes with: "I'm going to use frequency to mean how often does something happen."
> *d. The frequency of different score outcomes*
> The list of number-pairs is examined: "How often have you got a score of two?" "Once." The teacher does the same thing with the score of three. At the end of the report, the editors comment "And so it went on."

THE QUESTION

There seems to be no question about the content of this lesson: a well-known mathematical topic, that is, the beginnings of probability—outcomes in the range of various possibilities, frequency, score. The gentle progression from experience to figures and ideas, the demand for explanations and proof, the clear-cut definition of concepts is mathematics. But there remains a question which is unanswered: What does mathematics *mean* in this case? What does probability, outcome, pairs of numbers, frequency, and so on mean in the context set up by this lesson (and by the lessons that preceded it)? I am not asking for the ideas in the minds of the pupils, and I do not intend to look into their heads. What I want to do is to redefine the *wide field* in which one point or a small *corner* is defined in this lesson—seen as a set of acts by all the actors. I am interested in the process leading from the knowledge that is at everyone's disposal to the knowledge that is constituted and stated as valid in this particular lesson.

My interest derives from a central educational concern. Education has to aim at individual autonomy. That means that teaching must enable the young to recognize the possibilities of humankind as potentially their own, and to appropriate them. The larger the sector that is opened up by classroom work and the more the pupils are aware of their mobility in it, the more they can easily *move* in the field—the field being a metaphor of the socially constructed reality.[50] The contribution of school and school instruction to the children's gaining autonomy can be depicted as the opening of a field; that is, the *opening of possibilities for acting independently in their world*. It is for this reason that I will examine our lesson once more in spite of the fact that everything may have seemed to be clear on a first reading.

The first observation I have to make is that there is little information about the lesson's context. Maybe it is self-evident for British readers familiar with comprehensive schools, math teachers, unstreamed classes, and so on. They might understand the particular context without needing further information by placing their observations into the framework of a well-known context. Questions about these elements of the lesson's framework are unnecessary for our British reader, but for a person from Mars or a German educationalist, they are necessary questions.

What I can easily find out is that the comprehensive school was an important innovation in the British school system. Anybody could tell me that. But if I asked, "What is the place of dice in the children's everyday lives and what does 'dice' mean for them?" they might wonder what that has to do with our lesson. Information of this kind is not usually a part of our attempts to understand what has happened in the classroom, neither in Britain nor in Germany nor in the United States.[51] Nevertheless, I am going to ask my question of content in general and the dice in particular.

THE CHILDREN AND THE TEACHER

The authors give us some information about the class: "an unstreamed class of eleven- to twelve-year olds in a comprehensive school in a small market town." The teacher "had skillfully and sympathetically built up a climate of acceptance that encouraged participation." The lesson:

> . . . was part of a fortnight's work concerned with the mathematical treatment of situations in which exact results cannot be predicted but in which there may be general trends. The children had done a number of experiments, tossing coins, throwing

dice, and so on, and when this lesson started they already had some notion of how it is possible to say that when you throw a dice . . . a large number of times, about one-sixth of the throws will show a 1.

The children throw the dice. When I was an 11-year old child, whether I won or lost in Parcheesi depended on the throw of the dice. I knew the concepts of fair and loaded dice well, and I had an idea of probability. I had learned all this from playing Parcheesi. I also knew something about the way in which one concept is related to the other: When I had the impression that I had to wait too long for a 6, I suspected that one of the dice was loaded—mine or my partner's. That is my story from the 1940s; what about British children some 30 years later? I assume that these children also had a more or less clear knowledge of the topic of this lesson, derived from their practical experience outside the school. The lesson itself confirms this presupposition: The term "frequency" is familiar to all of the pupils; Gary even gives a kind of scientific explanation: "cycles a wave makes."

There is virtually no information about the teacher. Possibly he is regarded by the authors as an institution rather than a personality. He seems to be a math teacher. He obviously agrees with one of the aims of the comprehensive school in that he is concerned with creating a positive emotional climate in the classroom. That is all we know.

MATHEMATICS

The class is concerned with "probability" and earlier lessons have explored some of the foundations of probability. The result of this work was an empirically founded notion of probability: "about one-sixth of the throws will show a 1." Now the search is for all the possible outcomes when throwing two dice. The throw at the beginning of the lesson was an illustration rather than the starting point of an empirical approach to the topic. The teacher starts from the throws and then lets the children consider the problem in their minds.

Let us look at the results of their considerations. Ian said it "doesn't matter" how they choose to describe the outcomes, and all agreed. As a matter of fact it does— mathematically speaking! "6 and 1" is an *event*—the figures representing the top sides of the dice, nothing else. This is quite different from the *score* 7 (= 6 + 1)— the figures here being mathematical objects that can undergo certain defined operations, in this case addition. That "doesn't matter" mixes up both issues, which is reasonable only by presupposing a missing argument: By this "adding together," you define another event: "7" is the event defined by the simultaneous occurrence of, for example, a "6" and a "1" or of a "2" and a "5."

There is still another problem in this. During the second discussion on "the number of the possible outcomes" we read the following:

Gary:	Because there's six numbers on a dice and we've got two dice. You can have a one with a two, and keep on going. One three, one four, one five, one six. Then two one, two two, –
Teacher:	Did you say one three?
Pupil:	We've got that already.

And a bit later:

Ian:	. . . I think it's sixteen.
Teacher:	Why?
Ian:	Because . . . you're going to get six with one, aren't you?
Teacher:	Six pairs beginning with a one?
Ian:	Yes. So you've got all the other numbers. Then—er—the two. You're only going to get four different ones because—er—you have the rest in the six—in the one line.
Teacher:	Keep going. Come on.
Ian:	And then so on. And then with the threes, there's only going to be three because you have all the rest in the ones before.
. . .	
Ian:	And so on.
Teacher:	Ian's line. He says you can begin with the first column. There'll be six pairs in the first column. Then in the next column he thinks there'll be fewer. And then in the next column fewer still.

The editors add the information, which is quite relevant, "that each child had one red dice and one yellow." "What is on the board is three one. Is that the same [as the one three, we've got already], or isn't it?" That is exactly the point I want to make!

First of all it is not the same. A "yellow 6" is a different event to a "red 6," the difference between the two events being exactly the same as that between a "yellow 6" and, let us say, a "red 4." This difference is neglected by the pupil who says, "We've got that already"—and by Ian. Unfortunately we do not know whether or not the teacher agrees. The record ends at the very point where we could:

Teacher:	Now, how often have you got a score of three? (Pause) . . . How can you get a score of three with two dice?
Tony:	Two and one.
Teacher:	Two and one. Have you got that in your list somewhere?

How often have you got it? Can you get it? We are not told. Once? That would be in Ian's line. Twice? That would be in consequence with the two-dice issue—and with the usual textbook treatment of probability.

That leads us to a second point of view. A "6" as an arithmetical object is a 6, whether it is yellow or red. When you are going to score, color does not matter.

Mathematical operations such as addition abstract from color. In this respect Ian and the other pupil have done mathematics. By the way, it was Ian who made that remark, "It doesn't matter," when the teacher asked, "Which is the right way?" (that is, of describing the outcome).

In other words, in this lesson, there is mix-up between numbers as *mathematical objects* and numbers as labels for *events*. The lesson's subject is "the mathematical treatment of situations in which results cannot be predicted but in which there may be general trends"—in other words probability. The issue of probability stems from events, and probability aims at statements about the frequency of events. Our lesson begins with the listing of events. This context of the matter dealt with—outcome of throwing two dice simultaneously—is left unclear as long as "it doesn't matter" which way of describing the outcome is chosen.

There is evidence that the teacher knows all this very well. He brings up the matter by interrupting Gary; he does not answer the question for the number of different outcomes. Why, then, does he allow the mix-up?

THE DIDACTIC TRADITION

Perhaps there is a special didactic context to which the teacher's strategy corresponds—we are not told. Maybe there is a curriculum or a schoolbook or something similar that he is following or modifying—we are not told that either. If we knew, we could better understand the teacher's strategy. However, we can draw some conclusions from the comments given by the editors.

According to them, our teacher follows a "single-track" strategy. More precisely, the teacher brings the pupils from experience to figures and frequencies, from guesses to explanation, from his own reactions to the problem itself, from vague concepts to clear-cut definitions—in short, to mathematics by doing mathematics.

These comments have nothing to do with mathematics itself. The editors' argument is a *didactic* one. Obviously there is a strong didactic impact on the mathematical theme in this lesson. This impact matches quite well the information we have about the teacher. His actions in the classroom correspond to a didactic maxim that the editors offer in one of their comments, and that is agreed upon by half of the pedagogical world:

> Helping a pupil to work out his ideas . . . [and not to] turn a child's thought into his own, so that the child appears to produce an acceptable formulation but one which is really the teacher's and which leaves the child's meaning uselessly locked within him . . .

. . . or lost in the classroom, I add. This implies *not* assessing children's guesses or essays, but helping them to find out themselves whether they are right or wrong. This leads us to another aspect of the content of classroom.

THE VALIDITY OF KNOWLEDGE

Everybody producing knowledge, whether it is just a guess or a well-founded claim, makes a case for the validity of his or her knowledge. My questions are: What claim is made? and, Who are the authorities that legitimize the validity? First of all, there seems to be a claim to truthfulness. Let us have a look at this:

Teacher: ... which is the right way? Jane?
Jane: Saying separately.
Teacher: ... That's the right one to say, is it? Geoff?
Geoff: Hm. Add together. . . .
Teacher: ... So there are two ways of describing . . .

I agree with the editors who speak of "a guess at what the teacher wants." What the teacher did when *not* deciding the issue was to make a claim to truthfulness: Give your opinion and do not guess what another person might want to hear!

Secondly, there is a claim to truth. There were guesses at the beginning—the validity of which depended on the pupils' incomplete knowledge. But then they were brought to test their ideas by comparing the guesses to reality; that is, to the list of pairs produced under the logic of combination. The validity of this lesson's results depends on the pupils truthfulness and reason within the limits of the teacher's definition of what has to be done and what way they have to work.

From this we learn once more that mathematics as a discipline is not the authority that guarantees the validity of the knowledge worked out. If it is mathematics at all, it is—metaphorically speaking—refracted by the pedagogical authority represented by the teacher.

CONCLUSION

Let the ethnomethodologists (see p. 1) summarize his impressions. He takes the classroom for a world of its own. In our lesson, the activities were those of furnishing one small corner of this world. The furnishings that were put in place were "the outcomes of throwing two dice," "frequency," and "frequency of outcomes." It is up to the teacher to define the corner within the context of the surrounding world. To speak of a corner might be misleading: It is a world of its own that is established. As we saw, the connections with mathematics are somewhat difficult. And the link with the everyday lives of the children, or the life of the teacher, are no clearer.

The benefit of this separation of classroom from the life outside is that, in the pedagogical corner thus defined, the pupils can exercise observation and reasoning—with more or less guidance and more or less protection by the teacher against the oppressive complexity of the world as a whole. The cost is the risk of establishing a playroom in a doll's house rather than sketching out a sector that corresponds to the real world. That means in our case, as we saw, the risk of domination of subject matter by pedagogical concern.

Why do I explicate all this? My starting point was an analysis of subject matter, or the content of classroom. So, I could have confined myself to the propositions raised in the lesson, and I could have done something similar to a "content analysis." But I would not have grasped the "content" from a pedagogical point of view by doing that. I could have outlined the semantic fields to which the propositions of this classroom belong. But this would have raised the problem that instruction establishes a semantic field of its own and the question about the relation between both of them.

I wanted to avoid the shortcomings of empirical classroom research where either content is not looked into at all or there is a make-believe exactness behind which the complexity of subject matter disappears. I tried to avoid these pitfalls by reconstructing the context of content.

A German "observer" of this classroom might be allowed a final remark: Our lesson, as it is reported, has no attribute that gives it the flavor of a British classroom, except perhaps some pupils' names. There are classrooms like this one throughout Germany. This means that there are shared cultural traditions, particularly mathematical and pedagogical ones. The task of further discovery of these underlying cultural schemes and governing rules still remains.

8

The Formation of Conscience: A Lost Topic of Didaktik

> It's your job to change the pictures of the world.
> It's my job to change your world.
> —Gudmund Hernes, former Norwegian Minister
> of Church, Education, and Research

A FIRST APPROACH TO THE PROBLEM

The problem I will deal with in this chapter is well known within German Didaktik: the difference between knowledge and conscience. What does this mean? Let me introduce the problem by a story. Some years ago I read the following in a German journal:

A Roman Catholic parish wanted to give their minister a farewell present. They knew he would like figures of saints for his old church. In a vote, the members of the parish decided to get sculptures of the Nazi victims Edith Stein and Maximilian Kolbe. A sculptor was commissioned to present sketches. The sculptor's proposal for Edith Stein was agreed upon, but they hesitated with the naked Maximilian

Kolbe. They finally decided to realize the sculptor's plan. In the priest's final service the figures were revealed and blessed.

Soon afterward a bitter and rather unchristian fight was fought about the naked man in the local press. After some time the affair seemed to have calmed down. But one day the offensive sculpture was gone, stolen it seemed. But the sculptor believed that it was the work of iconoclasts. A woman from the village said: "The figure has been burned." If she was right, the sculpture and the real body would have been destroyed in the same way: burned in an oven.

From its beginnings, the problem of tolerance has not been an easy one for the Christian church: It is reported that St. Paul had to settle an argument within the young community in Corinth. Some of them did not think it wrong to eat meat slaughtered in a heathen rite as—for them—there were no other gods except the One. For others, eating meat was a nuisance. In those days there were no majority votes. So St. Paul appealed to the conscience of the first group not to offend the others. "If you are hurting their weak consciences, you will sin against Christ!" Those members of the Corinth community who were committed to tolerance by St. Paul would have had their own thoughts in the matter. His strong words show that he expected even more: They were to *follow* his advice and act tolerantly.

Whatever it is like in a Christian community, in education and in the classroom it is our obligation to develop tolerant students. We begin this work even with the little ones:

We teach our small pupils how toads live in forests and ponds; in an ecological balance with other animals and plants; occasionally protected by human beings when this balance is threatened. Can we—and how can we—make sure that our pupils will not go catching the toads (for now they know where to find them), pulling their legs off and slashing their bellies open instead of protecting them from car drivers and little rascals?

We convey knowledge, but that is not all. Something must be added which I call the *formation of the conscience*. It is in this sense that I speak of the "knowledge-conscience problem." It is a practical problem as my example shows.

But the knowledge-conscience problem has been lost, or at best submerged, in the German Didaktik of our days, though we can trace it far back in history:

- Johann Amos Comenius, in his didactical works, presupposed a unity of *scientia* and *conscientia* (knowledge and conscience).
- Johann Friedrich Herbart (1776–1841) introduced the frequently quoted term *erziehender Unterricht* (educative teaching).
- A variant of Herbart's term, which I will take up in this chapter, is the concept of *Bildung des Gewissens* (formation of conscience), used in the beginning of the 1960s by Josef Derbolav, who explicitly referred back to Herbart.

Derbolav expressed the problem of knowledge and conscience in the following way. In schools, "positive" knowledge about the world is imparted; that is, knowledge about actual facts and their relationship to the world we live in—let us say knowledge about the origin and the basic principles of the American Declaration of Independence, *and* the Declaration's binding character for the American political system. We assume that our pupils can actually benefit from this knowledge after the lesson, and even after they leave school. But how can we *guarantee* that a "theoretical insight into the world as our field of knowledge" implies a development of conscience, an imparting of "motives for action" within this world (Derbolav, 1960, p. 22)?

"Conscience" in this context is a code word for motives in general, understood not in a moralizing but rather in a moral way, not as an expression of a certain moral system but, rather, as an expression of an autonomous subject's responsibility—a subject who acts and accepts responsibility for his or her actions. Derbolav had no doubt that this conscience could be *formed*. But while we know that *reason* can be formed by means of knowledge, the question is, how can *conscience* be formed?

In other words, both acquisition of knowledge, which is an inevitable part of our dealing with the world, and acquisition of motives, which occurs in any event, should be the task of a school teaching which aims at contributing to the adolescents' maturity, that is, responsible and independent living in the world. Herbart had the same aims in mind. Indeed, virtually all educationalists agree on this purpose: The next generation should learn to master life in a humane way—a purpose that justifies education in general and the school in particular.

There is only one problem left: How can we realize this "both knowledge and conscience" in classroom work? In the following pages, I will explore some of the solutions that emerge when we look at German Didaktik.

AN ALL-TOO-SIMPLE SOLUTION: THE DIDACTIC INDICATIVE

There is a too-simple solution to the knowledge-conscience problem. When we look at the language of some textbooks and in teaching curricula, we may come to the conclusion that success of classroom work comes automatically, provided that we follow the suggested or advised method of teaching. This assumption is expressed in a sentence we often come across in teaching curricula: "The pupil learns . . . ." Didaktik discourse, whether within the framework of hands-on learning, open classrooms, or new ways of education in environmental problems, is often dominated by this—as I call it—"didactic indicative." There is no evidence at all that the classroom works as the "didactic indicative" indicates beyond, perhaps, age-old experience. It would be much different if the language went—more honestly—like this: "In suggesting this, we hope that the pupils will learn this or that," perhaps followed by, "It will have to be assessed, whether the desired success has been achieved." The didactic indicative makes things much easier.

In the training of teachers the didactic indicative has proved to be, to put it assertively, disastrous. Good intentions are passed off as reality. It is enough to "think school anew" (as Hartmut von Hentig, 1994, put it); the school will then change automatically and, above all, its pupils will change with it. Do they? We are not told. The ignorance about this simple question to which the didactic indicative leads is disastrous in Didaktik, too. Reflection on teaching stops halfway through—before we consider whether we have achieved certain educational objectives or whether teaching has made its contribution to the establishment of stable orientations as a guidance for students' lives within society. We have no reason to rely on an automatism, based on the principles of reform pedagogy, developmental psychology, or any other principles, to induce moral judgment in children after instruction.

The "Educational Objectives"

The problem we are exploring is the knowledge-conscience question. It is a problem that is, firstly, posed to didactical theory in order to secure an understanding and, secondly, a practical one, which is to be dealt with in the practice of teaching. But unfortunately, our problem is not an obvious one. Derbolav himself did not make it easy for his colleagues and students to understand what he was after, and he did not explain how he intended to deal with the problem in detail. And soon after his essay was published, the motivation to pursue the issue just disappeared. It is not mentioned as a problem in Herwig Blankertz's *Theories and Models of Didaktik* (1969).

Where did this problem disappear to? Assuming it is really as important as I suggest it is, should there not be something like a functional equivalent? There is one—and it comes in two variants, both of which can be identified in the literature as early as around 1960.

In 1962, Paul Heimann presented a structural analysis of teaching in order to disclose an "operational didactical field of reference" in the course of teacher training.

> Given that pupils in schools should become aware of situations, be affected by them, or realize something in them, we can divide teaching intentions into the following categories:

- The cognitive-active domain (knowledge, thoughts, basic convictions)
- The affective-sympathetic domain (feelings, experiences, beliefs)
- The pragmatic-dynamic domain (abilities, skills, habits, actions, completion of tasks)

In other words these are "possibilities of development to be found in human nature, which the activity of teaching has to orient on" (Heimann, 1970, pp. 127–128).

The development of beliefs and convictions as maxims of action are the constitutive elements of Heimann's view of instruction. Despite the lack of clarity in his terminology, there are certain parallels between his "convictions" and "beliefs" and the "conscience" introduced in a more traditional terminology by Derbolav.

As we all know, a short while later the second volume of the *Taxonomy of Educational Objectives* (Krathwohl, Bloom, & Masia, 1964) emerged as a means of classifying what Heimann called "intentions." However, instead of using the *Taxonomy* to define terms more precisely, a characteristic and momentous limitation of the awareness of the actual problem occurred in Didaktik as an outcome of the way the Taxonomy was used in Germany. The "affective domain" became an "*affektive Dimension*" in the process of translation. The everyday use of terms then led to the connotations of the word *Affekte*, meaning "emotions" or even "passions." As a consequence, there was no more talk about the "preference for a value," or of "characterization by a value," and the like.

Indeed, the terminology around the whole area was even further oversimplified—and this is still the case today—as the "affective domain" was defined in a negative way, by contrasting it with the "cognitive domain." Thus, today we hear many complaints about a "purely cognitively oriented teaching." The "affective domain" is then regarded as a necessary corrective, often making use of Pestalozzi's formula "head, heart, and hand." As a means of forming the heart—whatever that means—teaching procedures are suggested, especially those that grant freedom and a satisfying school life. The rest follows the didactic indicative; that is, it is supposed to work automatically.

Hands-on Learning

In the same year that Heimann developed his structural analysis, Klafki (1963) published an essay with the subtitle "The Problem of an Education Towards Responsibility." In view of the public "complaints about the lack of willingness to accept responsibility among young people," he declared that "a sense of responsibility," the willingness to "act in a responsible way or to accept responsibility for one's own actions" has to be regarded as a constitutive element of education. He proposed that both practical commitment and theoretical reflection could be means of "inducing the disposition to responsibility "(p. 49), and here again I see a functional equivalent to "conscience." Klafki suggests a solution—a partial abolition of school:

> Maturing towards the acceptance of responsibility is achieved within a complex situation: The adolescent temporarily leaves the protected area of school and takes up the challenge of real-life experience, commitment, responsibility and trial. He then returns to the protected area. In this respect . . . the school's task lies . . . in critical reflection on experience. (1963, p. 62)

One of the evidences Klafki gives to underline his argument is practical training courses incorporated into the curriculum of secondary schools. But these courses have had a somewhat sobering result, as Klafki had to admit. The commitment, the seriousness, and the stimulus of those practical tasks, intended to induce a feeling of responsibility in young people, were certainly there. What Klafki observed, on the other hand, was a lack of critical reflection, which was supposed to make the intended convictions available. The situative context of action is so complex that the tasks themselves are not clear anymore to the students. As a consequence, his considerations end with a characteristic argument, let me call it "schooling utopia":

> If the school is really serious about an education towards responsibility it has to alter or extend its traditional way of seeing itself. It cannot think of itself . . . as a relatively "protected area" any more, as an enclave for young people within the social-economical-political reality . . . . It has to . . . lead the adolescent temporarily to the experiences of fundamental interaction, commitment, and accepting responsibility in a reality *outside* school. (1962, p. 71, emphasis added)

And this results in something like cutting the Gordian knot:

> There should be no doubt that in the field of schools providing a general education, in the field of job training, night schooling, adult education, and teacher training important consequences regarding the theory of curricula and to methodology arise. (p. 71)

With this sword stroke of a new way of understanding (similar to that "thinking school anew") the picture of a new educational system seems to develop logically and automatically. However, educationalists are not politicians. And, since then, there has not been much change toward the practices urged on schools by Klafki.

In the Federal Republic of Germany of the 1980s, schooling utopias like the one outlined by Klafki gained many supporters. The motto was "hands-on learning." It no longer seemed necessary to leave the school for practical courses because it seemed possible to create contexts of action right in school. Let me give an example.

In his *Guide to Lesson Preparation*, Hilbert L. Meyer (1980), one of our Didaktik opinion leaders, reports on the following situation:

> In a teaching unit on agriculture several lessons were devoted to the topic of poultry farming. The aim was to compare the natural living conditions of hens with battery farming. In a first step the pupils and the five students who had planned and given this teaching unit together made life-size hens from old newspapers and much wall-paper paste. On the next day the class was split in two groups; the first group was to built a hen-house similar to natural living conditions, the second group was to make a battery-farm, oriented to the economic aspects.
>
> The first group then started to build their hen-houses with the help of the simplest things (a sponge was used as a bowl; a cardboard box as a coop; grass was fetched

from outside); they were finished within twenty minutes. In the meantime the second group was busy putting together cardboard boxes as batteries and then conjuring up two conveyor-belts with toilet-paper rolls; one for the food and one for clearing away the excrement. In a third step the pupils had a look at each others' work and discussed reasons for building their coops this or that and not another way. (pp. 213–214)

In Meyer's book the result of the pupils' work is given in pictures (see Figure 8.1). In their evaluation, the five students reported on this part of their practice teaching:

> While we had more or less concentrated on teacher-focused instruction in the first two weeks we now realized that the pupils had far more fun during the lessons, that their reactions were more spontaneous, and that they used their imagination. Some pupils, who had not actively participated in the lessons before, really seemed to unbend. We experienced the same. The lessons were not planned so much in advance any more, and there was room for spontaneity. Furthermore our teaching became more relaxed. By using different and—both for us and the pupils—new ways of teaching we succeeded in filling the pupils with enthusiasm for the topic of agriculture. (p. 215)

I will return to Meyer's lesson and his students' reactions later in this chapter. In all events there was no more talk about a sense of responsibility; and Derbolav's "motives of action" were reduced to "motivation," understood from a psychological point of view. "This is fun!"—that seemed to be the only important thing in Meyer's hen-battery report.

However, the moral commitment characteristic of didacticians' advocacy of the different varieties of hands-on learning has, I believe, roots in an unexpressed

Source: Meyer, 1980, p. 215.

FIGURE 8.1. Different ways of poultry farming.

hope that this kind of instruction will promote the formation of what we call "conscience. " I assume that they do not use this term because of its connection with particular moral traditions.

INTERIM RESULTS

As I have been suggesting, the formation of conscience is not a topic within today's Didaktik. Nevertheless I believe that, phrased in a different way, the problem of conscience was part of both the "educational objectives" movement of the 1970s as well as the orientation of teaching to the principle of action of the 1980s. In the following pages I would now like to suggest how the problem could be rediscovered for today's didactical *reflection*.

Let me stress an important point immediately: I am not aiming to produce a specific conscience for children and adolescents. I also do not seek means to implant historically based moral values. This would be indoctrination—and nobody wants that. My problem is the *formation* of a conscience, the cultivation of a moral authority within the young people, as it were, that enables them to see clearly the difference between good and evil, between use and abuse, and to choose one and condemn the other.[52]

USUS ATQUE ABUSUS—THE *ORBIS SENSUALIUM PICTUS* AND THE PRIMER

As I have emphasized in several places in this volume, Johann Amos Comenius's fame has its roots in his readers and, particularly, in his illustrated reader for little

FIGURE 8.2.   The "Fire," from Comenius's *Orbis Sensualium Pictus* (1978, pp. 12–13).

children, his *Orbis Sensualium Pictus*. (Comenius, 1978, originally published in 1658) Obviously this is far more than a contemporary picture book.

Let us take "The Fire" (see Figure 8.2). The figure shows words in Latin and German, and also things presented as illustrations. And what else? A story (see p. 117), and a story with a moral—an obvious moral, but not put into words. The story locates the place, which the thing that is described has in everyday life or, to put it more carefully, *should have* in everyday life. When looking at the picture and reading the story we are obliged to take care of the fire *without* any argument being made to compel, or even persuade, us to do so. The picture and story tells us what to do and what to avoid. *Usus atque abusus*, use and abuse, are shown in Comenius's book—but by the choice of stylistic means and by their arrangement in these compositions.

Now let us take *our* primers—the letters are embedded in stories; or take arithmetic texts—the figures are incorporated in everyday situations (see Figures 8.3 and 8.4). Susanne and Alexander have to learn that $5 - 1 = 4$ and that $4/2 = 2$. At one and the same time, they learn that they are able to—*and have to*—peacefully divide the candy Anette brought them.

Or let us recall that fine example of Meyer's hen battery (see Figure 8.1). I am convinced that Meyer's students had intended to evoke certain feelings of "good" (picture a) and of "bad" (picture b) in their pupils. I am also convinced that Meyer himself selected his example to do more than demonstrate hands-on

Source: Eisenlohr, 1995, p. 25

FIGURE 8.3.   From a German Primer: The letters "au," "s," "sz," "st."

Source: Büttner, Rose, & Teichmann, 1937, p. 2

FIGURE 8.4.   From a German arithmetic book.

learning. He aimed to induce in his readers an awareness of environmental issues and to create the conditions for a value judgment—without an artificial moral, but by merely looking at the pictures or the products of the children's work.

We can find many other illustrations of this kind in the field of environmental education. There are fine examples of effective compositions, but there are also examples of compositions that do not seem to have the desired effect, and to which an artificial moral has been added (see Figure 9.9). But one thing is missing. The inventors of these nice examples do not seem to fully understand what they are doing.

A CONSENSUS ON THE GOOD

I will now explore what happens in the cases I described earlier. To do so, I will go back to Derbolav's "levels of reflection" because, to my mind, it does allow us to clarify the issues:

- Susanne and Alexander start school. They learn about natural numbers, and fractions. These *numbers* are there only for calculations, and calculation is only done with numbers. Numbers as such do not really have anything to do with sharing candy.
- However, the *story* in the arithmetic book, the veiled arithmetic problem, directs attention back to everyday life, where numbers and calculations *are* an aspect of sharing; for example, "sharing" means dividing amounts and quantities among individuals.

Numbers—or whatever the topic of a lesson might be—*contain* a part of, or an aspect of, ways of dealing with everyday life, of human interaction. They *contain* an aspect of social practice. This means, on the one hand, that the practice is not made visible explicitly, it cannot be experienced directly; on the other hand, it means that the practice of dividing is included in the notion of "fractions." It is the aim of the primers' authors to establish, or to reestablish, the connection between school subjects and social practice.

However to this point we have not dealt with the formation of conscience. It takes more to do that. Derbolav uses the long-winded phrases, "specific normative structures, implied in the contents" and the "norms worked out by the self in the educational situation, whereas at the same time a certain individually structured horizon of responsibility is gained" (Derbolav, 1960, pp. 27–28). How are we to understand this?

Everyday life is, furthermore and before all, guided by a consensus of what is good and bad. This consensus is not so much like the Ten Commandments'

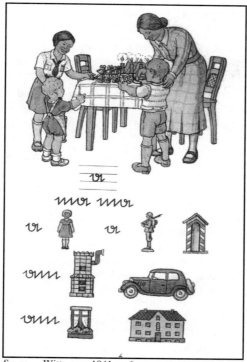

Source: Wittmann, 1941, p. 6

FIGURE 8.5. From a German primer:
The letters "a," "am," "ma," "ma ma."

"thou shalt" but rather a "we do things, or things are done, in this or that way."[53] This consensus can be reconstructed from the compositions and stories in the *Orbis Pictus* as well as from Johann Bernhard Basedow's *Elementarwerk* (1909, originally published in, 1770) and from my Nazi primer of 1941 (see Figure 8.5[54]).

A COMPULSION TO THE GOOD?

What is good is given and not deliberately imposed by mere will, and even by a didactician's will. But, how can we methodically form the conscience, and, more particularly, in a way that guides human actions:

- Without the presence of physical force
- Without treating it as the consequence of a formal syllogism
- Without simply imposing moral principles; and, above all
- Without leaving the whole matter to the individual's sense of acting responsibly—which is to be provoked, first of all, by teaching?

This is a didactician's, that is, our, question. Let me try to answer it.

To begin with, I refer to teachers in their classrooms. They know quite well how to do their job. What do they do? They *tell stories* and *compose pictures*, simple ones at the beginning, more complex ones later on. And they methodically *arrange classrooms* in such a way that the product of classroom work is convincing to the pupils' minds, so that they are prepared to willingly act in a humane way in the outside world.

It was Herbart who conceptualized the logic of such practice in his famous essay on "The Aesthetic Presentation of the World Being the Main Duty of Education," originally published in 1804. He argues as follows (Herbart, 1964):

> Education has to aim at morality. That means [within in the terms of Herbart's psychology] that human inclinations have to be governed by will. What kind of judgment can convince the will to strive for the Good? The judgment in question cannot be a logical one as we do not look for logical consequences. Our aim is the constitution of a personality acting on moral principles and not the logical derivation of moral consequences. (p. 105)

The only judgment remaining is the aesthetic judgment:

> Among all sorts of necessities for convincing [the will] there remains only the aesthetic necessity. It can be characterized as being able to create categorical judgments without any proof and without any kind of force. It is indifferent with regard to inclinations. And it develops from the perfect imagination of its object. (p. 110)

Herbart continues his argument this way:

> When a human finds a fundamental and practical, i.e., aesthetic necessity, a person, acting on the basis of moral principles, will direct its inclination to give obedience to it [that is, that necessity]. . . . [This self-reflection is possible] in so far as the self finds the very inclination contained *within the object* of the aesthetic judgment *within itself*, too. (p. 111, emphasis added)

But with the logic of different kinds of judgment, Herbart leads us into the depths of the philosophy of aesthetics and *Bildung*. I have already explored these issues and I do not want to reopen them here. Let us go back to our didactical task instead—just as Herbart himself does in this essay. First of all he supports "reading the Odyssey with boys." After that he thinks of all those "characters who enter the course of history, each of them illuminated if possible by his classic chronicler. Periods not described by a master and not inspiring a poet are worth very little in education" (p. 118). This is the neohumanistic educational philosophy at the heart of even the modern German Gymnasium.

So it was not by chance that Derbolav worked out Herbart's idea in his 1957 book, *The Example As a Principle of Education in the Gymnasium.* And it is examples that I have been dealing with: stories, compositions, aesthetic creations in the broadest sense. In Chapter 6, I write more generally of the symbolic representation of reality, which we now can translate into the language of the classroom. When stories are told, pictures are drawn, compositions produced, and settings arranged, classroom work is work on the symbolically coded everyday life of the students.

The only question remaining is how to create the moral judgment. I can only answer this question as a didactician and not as a psychologist, and I will not go into great detail. Anyway the story that is told and the picture of the world that is drawn include readers and viewers in their worlds. Moreover, they invite, or rather urge us, without compulsion to take over the maxims of the persons acting in the stories and pictures as it were. To achieve this, one condition must be fulfilled, namely that we appear in the pictures and compositions. However, this does not suffice. It is, to return to Meyer's poultry farming, quite rare that a pupil is the daughter of a farmer and helps her parents to feed the chickens. What does this objection mean for our knowledge-conscience problem?

BRINGING THINGS TOGETHER

Let me now try to bring the threads of this account, that is, the notions of knowledge and conscience, together.

A play ends with the applause. Classroom work does not end with the end of the story. It is the end of the story that defines the starting point of classroom work. The classroom presentation of stories and pictures is followed by work. In the widest sense, stories and pictures are interpreted, but what does "interpretation" mean here? It means the work by which we bring together the two worlds, namely *the world of the story* told on the one hand *and the life-world of the students* on the other.

How does this work in detail? Instead of an explicit argument, let me present a picture (Figure 8.6) and tell a story[55]:

A "whining school-boy" in 1941 might have felt a strong desire to become a "soldier, jealous in honor" (Shakespeare, *As You Like It*) and fight battles against our enemies with mighty things like planes and cruisers. Susanne and Alexander sailed to Oslo with their parents in 1982. They read about the fate of the cruiser *Blücher*; they looked out for the battery of Oscarsborg which sank it; they helped their father to dip the ensign at the sight of the grave of more than 1,000 soldiers; they visited Fort Åkershus and the exposition that documents the German occupation of Norway; and they discussed the whole matter in great detail. I am sure that since then they *feel* things like war, occupation and resistance, death, and the ecological time-bomb (because of the ammunition in that grave) when regarding pictures such as the one given in Figure 8.6. And I hope that, accordingly, they come to a moral conclusion of disgust concerning the objects the pictures refer to. In short, their aes-

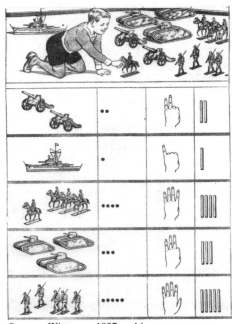

Source: Wittmann, 1937, p. 14

FIGURE 8.6.   From a German arithmetic book.

thetic judgment and their motives might differ somewhat from the naive one of their father in 1941.

Knowledge is indispensable for an adequate interpretation of the pictures. And the aesthetic presentation is indispensable to provoke strong motivations toward the knowledge they carry of what to do and how to do it.

A FINAL RESULT?

German didacticians will inevitably make the following objection to my argument as a whole: telling stories and composing pictures! That implies the risk of manipulation. Maybe that they are right. My answer to this is that the classroom is neither a stage nor TV. Stories and pictures are presented together with a *task*, and the presentations are followed by the pupils' *work*.

The lessons of Meyer's students began with an introduction about how hens live. This story provoked pictures the pupils already had in their minds. This was the beginning of the lesson and the *beginning* of a working process that *resulted* in a more appropriate and more complex conception of the world, or at least of poultry farming.

So, the didactician's next job is to reconstruct the structures of the double-sided process in the classroom, the process of the production of a product and, at the

Schola.

Die Schul 1
ist eine Werkstat/in welcher
die jungen Gemüter
zur Tugend geformet wer-
(den

Schola 1
est officina, in quâ
novelli animi
ad Virtutē formantur

Die Schul.

FIGURE 8.7. "The School," from
Comenius's *Orbis Sensualium Pictus* (1978, pp. 198–199).

same time, of the formation of mind and conscience. In Chapter 9, I will approach such a reconstruction.

The knowledge–conscience problem that I have sought to address is as follows: Classroom knowledge is conveyed, elaborated, and acquired; but what about the motives that guide our actions *outside* the classroom? Thus, knowledge is not something on its own; it refers to humans and their lives and actions in the world. Knowledge refers to everyday life where we know without question what is good and bad and act accordingly. When we consider this, we see that classroom work is more than simply the transport of "knowledge" from the teacher's into the students' heads. First of all, the conscience is informed, as it were, by the knowledge and the everyday situations it discloses to it; for example, the world of agricultural production and thus the "love of animals" can acquire form and context. Secondly, the students and their knowledge can be involved into the context that this knowledge opens up.

So, the work of the teacher is to compose a living "aesthetic presentation" that:

- on the one hand presents the subject matter correctly and in a sufficiently differentiated way; and
- on the other hand opens up a horizon of conscientious and conscience-guided acting.

Let me make a final remark. More than once I have talked about a consensus. But it might be argued that a consensus does not exist any more. I am not sure about that. But what is certain is that, if the consensus means to look after one's own interests only, one cannot expect the knowledge–conscience problem to be noticed at all, let alone that education and classroom will succeed in forming (*Bildung*) the conscience. As Comenius puts it (Figure 8.7), "School is the workshop where young souls are formed to virtue."[56]

9

Bild, Bildung, Weltbild

A THESIS

The title of this chapter, and the theme that I will be exploring, rests on a pun that is only possible in the German language: *Bild* ("picture" and "image" as well) and *Bildung*. But in reality it is not a pun: *Bild* and *Bildung* are etymologically closely related and the meaning of *Bildung* has to do with "picture" and "image"—as I will show in this chapter. *Weltbild* has been introduced into the philosophical jargon of English, and I would like to demonstrate that this term is also part of my theme, a kind of third player in the game.

In this chapter, I will only mention *Bildung* in passing; I discussed that term in Chapter 2. But I will be considering Comenius's *Orbis Sensualium Pictus* again as well as the copperplates of the *Elementarwerk* (Elementary Work) by Johann Bernhard Basedow. I will be examining their pictures from the vantage point of the claim that *in education, and especially in the classroom, we convey a* Weltbild—*that is, an image of the world by using pictures* (Bild) *and stories—and in this way contribute to the students'* Bildung. Both the *Orbis Sensualium Pictus* and the *Elementarwerk* differ fundamentally in the *Weltbild* they want to convey, but it *is* a *Weltbild* that underlies each series of pictures. Any textbook of our days could illustrate the point I want to make. But for me, the distance in time makes things more clearly visible.

BILDUNG

In Chapter 2, I introduced *Bildung as the process in the course of which specific human beings acquire the characteristic human features.* Now I ask: Is it possible to offer the whole world as a means of education, as an object for an individual human being? The attempt has been made from time to time. I will only mention one such attempt—perhaps the most famous one—and one that encouraged Basedow to develop his *Elementarwerk*. From 1750 to 1780, Jean Lerond d'Alembert and Denis Diderot edited the famous *Encyclopédie, ou Dictionnaire raisonné des sciences, des arts et des métiers* (Encyclopedia or Dictionary of the Sciences, the Fine Arts, and the Crafts—Founded in Reason). The *Encyclopédie* consists of a series of articles arranged in alphabetical order, but their choice of topics followed a highly sophisticated theory of knowledge. Where necessary one or more illustrations were added to the articles. According to d'Alembert and Diderot, their *Encyclopédie* was "a general image of the achievements of the human mind in every field and in every century" (Diderot, 1969, p. 37).

As a matter of fact, the *Encyclopédie* accomplishes even more:

> Thus we thought that it would be important to have a dictionary which one could consult for all matters concerning the fine arts and the sciences and which could guide those who feel themselves encouraged to enlighten those who learn by themselves.
>
> We conclude that the dictionary will contribute to the reliability and to the progress of the humankind's knowledge. And by multiplying the number of real scholars, of outstanding artists, and of enlightened amateurs it will spread out new opportunities in society.[57]

By this—enlighten others who learn by themselves—they indicate clearly that their aim is an educational one. Thus, they provide their readers (that is, the general public), with a means for a collective education.

PICTURES AND STORIES

Let me return to the idea of educating an individual, an education covering everything a human being needs in this life—and, in Comenius's world-view, in life after death. The question that has to be asked is: What is necessary for this life? To explore this question, let us look at the two picture books: the *Orbis Sensualum Pictus* by Comenius, a religious encyclopaedist of the early Enlightenment, and the *Elementarwerk* by Basedow, the oldest of the educational "philanthropists" and Immanuel Kant's "enlightened" contemporary. Both of these books have much in common, for instance:

- The great importance they ascribe to *nature* and, accordingly, the importance they give to the *study of nature*
- Nature, for lack of anything better, is made available in *pictures,* in Basedow's words, as "The Book of Nature"
- Their interest in *art* and particularly in *crafts*
- The interest in being able to *master* everyday life by the means of *knowledge* of the world

And, they also share an *epistemological empiricism* with the encyclopedists of the *Encyclopédie,* and with many other encyclopedic undertakings of their time.

Now I will turn my attention to the specific logic of representation, the logic of the sequence of the pictures and their contents, and the logic of the links of pictures with the explanations, or rather stories, presented alongside them. It is this logic, I want to reconstruct within the scope of the concept of *Bildung.* In this discussion, I will develop the following four observations:

1.   The books are explicitly *pedagogically framed.*
2.   There is an *order* according to which the matter is presented.
3.   There is an underlying conviction of how humankind has to make *use* of the world.
4.   This conviction is obviously in correspondence with the *society* in which the respective authors live.

JOHANN AMOS COMENIUS'S
ORBIS SENSUALIUM PICTUS (1658)[58]

1. Johann Amos Comenius's *Orbis Sensualium Pictus* is explicitly *framed didactically* through an *invitatio* (that is, an invitation) containing a picture at the beginning of the text, a *clausula* (that is, conclusion) at the end containing the very same

TABLE 9.1.   **Invitatio and Clausula from Comenius's *Orbis Sensualium Pictus***

	Invitatio		Clausala
T:	Come here boy! Learn wisdom.	*T:*	Now you've seen, in short, all the things conceivable and you have learned the most important words of the (Latin) German language. Go on like this and read diligently other good books, so that you will become educated, wise and pious.
P:	What is that?		
T:	To understand rightly, to do rightly, to pronounce rightly, all that is necessary.		
P:	And who is going to teach me that?		
T:	I am, with the help of God.		

Source: Comenius, 1978, p. 2, 309.

Invitatio.   **Einleitung.**

FIGURE 9.1.   "Invitatio," from Comenius's *Orbis Sensualium Pictus* (1978, p. 2).

picture, and a corresponding story as we see in Figures 9.1 and 9.2. The text that accompanies the pictures reads as shown in Table 9.1:

2. Within this didactical framing the *content* itself is framed as follows: The book begins with God (Figure 9.3) and His creation; the last picture is the Last Judgment (Figure 9.4); and the content of the book can be grouped as in Table 9.2.

Clausula.

Beschluß.

FIGURE 9.2.   "Clausula," from Comenius's *Orbis Sensualium Pictus* (1978, p. 308).

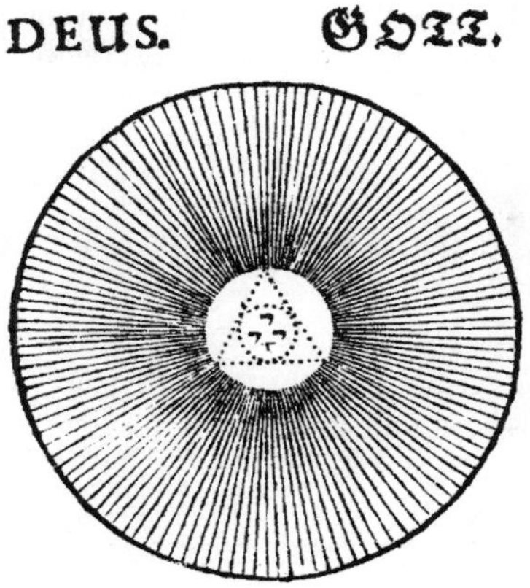

DEUS.   GOTT.

FIGURE 9.3.   **"God," from Comenius's *Orbis Sensualium Pictus* (1978, p. 6).**

"God" and the "Last Judgment" stand for the theoretical framework that opens up the themes of Comenius's primer in detail. A convincing example of the iconographic means he uses is the one seen in three pictures presented in Figure 9.5: He portrays the "world" by referring iconographically to the Genesis as God's creation; he introduces "human beings" with a depiction of the Fall of Man, which

Judicium Extremum.

Das Jüngste Gericht.

FIGURE 9.4.   **"The Last Judgment," from Comenius's**
Orbis Sensualium Pictus (1978, p. 306).

TABLE 9.2. Table of Contents of Comenius's
***Orbis Sensualium Pictus* (1978)**

God
    World–Heaven
    (Nature):
      • The 4 Elements: Fire–Air–Water–Earth
      • Flora and Fauna
    Human:
      • Crafts–Arts
      • Ethics–Society–State–Religions
    Predestination
Last Judgment

corresponds to the Genesis; and he also repeats a nearly congruent detail from the picture of the world's creation when he depicts "the outer limbs."

The order of God's Creation constitutes the order on which Comenius based his *Orbis Pictus*. So, what the book depicts is indeed an *orbis* (circle): the world as a circle, portrayed as God's creation and arranged according to God's order of creation and salvation.[59] This order is represented and conveyed mainly by iconographical means. Thus, pictures—and stories—are not a one-to-one illustration *of* the world but an illustration *of how* the readers, and observers, of the *Orbis Pictus* are supposed to see and *understand the world*.

Thus, we see that Comenius's point of view, which we can reconstruct from the *Orbis Pictus,* is humankind from the beginning (the Creation of the world), to its end (the Last Judgment). He presents the knowledge that opens up possibilities of living humanely in this world.

Homo.

Der Menſch.

FIGURE 9.5. The order of God's creation, from Comenius's
***Orbis Sensualium Pictus* (1978, pp. 8, 74, 78).**

FIGURE 9.6.   Details from the "Fire," from Comenius's
***Orbis Sensualium Pictus* (1978, p. 12–13).**

3. The knowledge Comenius offers is not only knowledge of *what* the world *is like*: The *Orbis Pictus* also tells us what human life within the world *should be like*. We can identify this feature if we take a closer look at one of the pictures. Let us look once more at the "Fire" (see Figure 8.2). What can we see? Comenius does not only give us a picture; his page contains also words in Latin and German:

> The fire burns and scorches. Its spark, resulting from steel hitting a flint stone or in a lighter, caught by tinder, ignites at first the sulfur thread and then kindles the candle or the wood and causes a flame or even a blaze which destroys houses.

These are words and pictures as representations of real objects. But it is not only words and things. In addition, things are arranged in a composition, a picture (*Bild*); and the words tell a story. Both—picture and story—have an obvious moral, a moral that is not, however, put into words. The picture and the story locate the place which the thing described has and should have in everyday life. Let me show that with some details from the "Fire" (see Figure 8.2 and Figure 9.6).

Usus atque abusus, use and abuse, are shown in these pictures and in the corresponding stories—without moral reasoning, but simply by the choice of stylistic means and by their arrangement in both these compositions. We are obliged to take care of the fire *without* any argument compelling—or even persuading—us to do so.

Thus, the *Orbis Pictus* gives the things as they are and, at the same time, the way they are to be used—or the things as we see them and the way we have to use them. This assumption is usually put as the concept of the identity of *scientia* and *conscientia*, a pun in both Latin and German but which again cannot be readily translated into English: the identity of knowledge and conscience. That means that a correct and thorough knowledge of the world implies—in the sense of formal logic—acting rightly in the world.

4. Finally, neither *scientia* nor *conscientia* is timeless. The order of creation only *seems* to be universal and beyond history; there is a picture—which is not however part of the *Orbis Pictus*—that is often called upon, because it shows Comenius's social context (see Figure 4.2). It is the reality of an early bourgeois society of the Bohemian Brethren—Comenius was their last bishop. In short, we may read the order I have reconstructed from the *Orbis Sensualium Pictus* as interrelated with a *specific* stage of the development of the bourgeois society. In other words, in his *Orbis Pictus,* Comenius conveyed a picture of the world, a *Weltbild.* And this *Weltbild* was correlated to the society in which he lived.

THE COPPERPLATES OF JOHANN BERNHARD BASEDOW'S ELEMENTARWERK (1787)

1. Johann Bernhard Basedow's *Elementarwerk* (Elementary Work) consists of two major parts. The first part is a textbook for educators, that is, parents and teachers—he thought of private teachers in a noble or a bourgeois family. This part begins with a "Short introduction into the techniques of education" which, as the title shows, presents the didactical framework of the whole. The second part is

FIGURE 9.7.   The end of human life, from Basedow's *Elementarywerk*
(1909, Tab. XCVI).

a collection of copperplates that were designed by the famous engraver and painter Daniel Chodowiecki. These pictures were produced for an explicitly didactical purpose. In the very first plate (see Figure 4.4), there is a nice example of how Basedow—and the "philanthropists," the group of educators he was associated with—thought about their teaching method, their "socratic-catechetic" method which I discussed in Chapter 4.

2. The series of pictures in Basedow's *Elementarwerk* starts with the picture of (as I would describe it) a bourgeois kitchen-cum-living room, stylized as the place where children—shown at four different ages—grow up. But in contrast to this first picture, let us look at the last picture—the end of human life, transferred into the language of Greek mythology (see Figure 9.7)[60]: We see Pluto (together with Persephone and the three judges faced with the appearance of a "ghost, dejected and charged by the sin" (Basedow, 1909, p. 35). What we see is *human life*, between birth and death, forming the framework for the series of pictures.

I will also add another small detail from the pictures, namely the order of the plates XXV to XLV: house—place with houses—plan of a town (Copenhagen)—country (Denmark)—Europe—the continents Asia, Africa, and Australia—world map—Germany.[61] Increasingly broad horizons are opened until one's eyes are cast back on the *individual's* own country.

Now let us return to the framework and to what it is framing. Looking at the series of pictures in detail, it is not easy to reconstruct an order. But let us look at the *Elementarwerk's* first part, that is, at the book and its table of contents (see Table 9.3). The first item indicates explicitly the pedagogical framing of the whole. What follows are headings for what *we know about the world*, arranged in a way that was usual in a school curriculum in the 18th century. Thus, the *Elementarwerk's* content reflects the same philosophy that underlies the *Encyclopédie*.

Basedow's point of view, which we can reconstruct, is human life between birth and death and he collects the knowledge that is at human disposal—on an "elementary" stage.

TABLE 9.3.   Table of Contents of Basedow's *Elementarwerk* (1909)

Content of the Elementary book

(Short introduction into the techniques of education)

About various things.
  Especially about humans and their minds

The commonly useful logic

About religion

Ethics

About occupations and classes of the people

Elements of history

Knowledge of nature

Further knowledge of nature

The essential grammar and rhetoric

FIGURE 9.8. Mistakes through which children ruin their clothes, detail from Basedow's *Elementarwerk* (1909, Tab. III).

  3. The pictures in Basedow's book are also based on the idea of a specific order in which it is spelled out how things belong together and how they are to be used. As an example, let us look at a detail showing fire (see Figure 9.8). When this pic-

FIGURE 9.9. Bad habits and generosity,
from Basedow's *Elementarwerk* (1909, Tab. II).

ture is compared to the one by Comenius, the radical change of perspective becomes obvious—it is a child's perspective.

Furthermore, the implicit moral of the pictures is not as straightforward for Basedow (and for his fellow philanthropists) as it was for Comenius. Thus, as a rule, the philanthropists insisted on adding an explicit moral to their pictures, for example, by headings such as those in Figure 9.9. And as a matter of fact, no one realizes (that is, without an explanation) that the latter shows "bad habits of some children at the table; generosity of two people toward a poor man."

Maxims such as this are explicitly added by Basedow in his explanation. All these stories, which were written for children by the philanthropists, and which are today very difficult to read sympathetically, conclude with an unmistakably formulated moral, a maxim for acting rightly. Nevertheless, as in Comenius's *Orbis,* the conjunction of pictures and stories is based on an assumption, namely of a more or less firm connection of *scientia* and *conscientia*—which may remind us once more to the knowledge-conscience problem discussed in Chapter 8.

4. The notion of "good" and "bad" the *Elementarwerk* implies is not timeless, although the philanthropists—and Basedow with them—share Jean Jacques Rousseau's epoch-making promise: to bring up a newborn as a *human* being *out-side* the borders of society and any particular class or profession. Their idea of education is a thoroughly bourgeois one. This is obvious when we look, for example, at Figure 9.9. But it is not only that.

Thus, when we compare Figure 9.8 with Comenius's "Fire"—see Figure 8.2— iconographic similarity as well as a rupture in the underlying philosophy is obvious. By such a juxtaposition of Comenius's *Orbis* and Basedow's *Elementarwerk,* I have been suggesting that there is no universally valid order as a basis for the two sets of illustrations. We do see an *order* in Basedow's work, but it is now—explicitly—no longer the order of God's creation. "Nature" has replaced God's creation; and it is nature that humankind—more precisely an enlightened bourgeois class—has recognized and that humans are able to recognize.

To sum up: Basedow, by means of Chodowiecki's copperplates and by his text conveyed a picture of the world, a *Weltbild.* It differs from that of Comenius. But nevertheless it is a *Weltbild* and it corresponds to the society he lived in.

BREAK AND CONTINUITY

In his interpretation of the two school-picture books we have been considering, Otto Friedrich Bollnow (1960) has emphasized that a "Copernican turn" has taken place between them: "Comenius's cosmic order" has changed into "a subjective human order." "Somewhere between Comenius and Basedow is a crucial break in our intellectual history: the loss of an objective order" (pp. 150–152). I think Bollnow's interpretation may be misleading. It is not the case that a "cosmic," an objective, order has been lost—as an objective order it never existed. But Bollnow's argument actually is two in one: it is about *order* and it is about a *specific* order. We would better speak of continuity—with respect to order—*and* of a break.

As we could see, many of the pictures of Basedow and Chodowiecki *resemble* those of the *Orbis Sensualium Pictus*, if we disregard the difference in style. Nevertheless we are looking at a completely *different* world. Although the engravers of the *Orbis* and the *Elementarwerk* make use of the *same* iconographic means in, for example, their respective last picture (see Figures 9.4 and 9.7), they embed their engavings in entirely *different* ideologies. There is a break—there is no doubt about this. The place of the *ordo salutis*—the order of salvation—is taken by the *curriculum vitae humanae*—the life of a human being within the world. There is the break as result of the movement of Enlightenment. But my intention has not been not to demonstrate this break—that has been done many times. It would be much more interesting to show how and under which circumstances the development from a theocentric to an anthropocentric *Weltbild* took place, which I have sketched in this chapter using the frames provided by Comenius and Basedow. This development came to an end at the beginning of our century when Ellen Key (1900) proclaimed the "century of the child." It is a development from the introduction to the context of the world created by God, expressed by the *Orbis Pictus,* to the individual and his or her education, a thought we found in Basedow's pictures.

But on the other hand we have seen—with the help of our pictures—a shared basic conviction in both our books—and in both our periods—and that there *is* an order according to which human life has to be organized. Pictures and stories:

- Represent this order in a symbolic way
- Are presented in a didactical context in such a way that pupils are able to recognize themselves in the stories and in the pictures. They can place themselves therein, and find themselves introduced into this order without force; and they
- Demand validity for the underlying order and the behavioral norms embedded in the respective order

Thus, however much the pictures of Comenius and Basedow differ in content, form and quality, their *function is the same*: The authors, as well as the engravers, pursue a didactical aim. They show *pictures* and tell *stories*. In doing so, they draw a particular image of the world, a *Weltbild*. This *Weltbild* is the framework of what nowadays we call *Bildung* of the youth—which enables me to pick up the pun of my topic.

CONCLUSION

At a time when the "loss of an objective order" (Bollnow, 1960, p. 151)[62] is earnestly discussed, when the lack of a binding orientation seems to give every reason for worry by educationalists, and when, with a postmodern attitude, things are left to individual discretion, it may be helpful to remember the topic of the identity of *scientia* and *conscientia*. There have been times when knowledge of the world was supposed, with a nearly logical necessity, to imply motives to act rightly. The *Orbis Sensualium Pictus* virtually offers itself as a proof for that and a reference to it may look like a search for a lost paradise. What I have suggested here is that nothing is lost. A firm and working order is always assumed; and it can be reconstructed, as I did it in the cases of Comenius and Basedow. And contemporary didacticians speaking of *Bildung* of the youth claim for an order of things and of knowledge, too.

Our two classical educationalists were not the only ones we could have called on: My two examples are simply special cases, cases that document the emergence of "education of youth" as a specific task for professional "educators." And today, we find books like the *Orbis Sensualium Pictus*, or at least like some of its chapters, in our schools as primers and reading books. It would be a rewarding task to analyze all those many editions, or rather revised versions, that have derived from the *Orbis Pictus*. In all of the books that either directly reinterpret the *Orbis Pictus* or draw knowingly or unknowingly on its inspiration, the pictures that are drawn and the stories that are told teach the children how the world and things in the world correlate. They convey a judgment about what is true and what is false and *at the same time* they convey an opinion about good and evil—whether they intend to do so or whether it happens by itself.

Notes

1. As an outcome of the work of this group, three collections of papers in English have appeared exploring the relationship between curriculum and Didaktik: Hopmann, S., & Riquarts, K. (Eds.). (1995). *Didaktik and/or curriculum* Kiel: Institut für die Pädagogik der Naturwissenschaften an der Universität Kiel; and Hopmann, S., & Gundem, B.B. (Eds.). (1998). *Didaktik and/or curriculum: An international dialogue.* New York: Peter Lang; and Westbury, I., Riquarts, K. & Hopmann, S. (Eds.). (2000). *Teaching as a reflective practice: The German Didaktik tradition.* Mahwah, NJ: Lawrence Erlbaum Associates.

2. See Hopmann and Riquarts (1995). It is interesting in this context that the index of the *International Encyclopedia of Education* (Husén & Postlethwaite, 1994) contains only one reference to the German Didaktik tradition: a one-page subtopic in the entry "Curriculum History: National Profiles."

3. Thus, even when there are accepted translations of some of the most basic terms in the German discussions, for example, of the kind found in every German-English dictionary, the actual German often refers to what are really different phenomena and concepts than their English counterparts. Thus, the German *Bildung* is not "education," although that is the most obvious and convenient direct translation; *Unterricht* is not "instruction," although that is the conventional translation; *Lehrplan* is not the American "curriculum" or the English "syllabus." And, of course, *Didaktik* is not "didactic." Conversely, "instruction" is not *Unterricht*, and so on.

So what should a writer seeking to present a "German argument" do? One solution is to highlight the difference by using, for example, *Didaktik* or *Bildung* (with or without italics) rather than *curriculum and instruction* or *education*. But that move only dramatizes the problem of cross-cultural interpretation; it does not solve it. And to routinely use a more appropriate translation such as, for example, "formation" for *Bildung* or "classroom work" for *Unterricht*, does not solve the problem ("formation" and "classroom work" are unusual usages in English-language educational discussions) but does have the merit of underlining the conceptual issues raised by the German framework. Menck defines the terms he uses by explaining, and then using, them.

4.   I am drawing heavily in this discussion on the experiences in the "Didaktik meets Curriculum" working group to highlight the issues that most vexed the conversations and formal meetings.

5.   The three-column format for lesson planning widely used in Germany and Scandinavia has, as headings for the three columns of the lesson plan, "What, "How," and "*Why*."

6.   It should be noted that this was also John Dewey's understanding of the relationship between "teaching" and the development of students (see Dewey, 1916, p. 25). Peter Menck has reminded me that Dewey had learned some of his lessons from German educational theory—while, in their turn, many German reform pedagogues learned from Dewey.

7.   See Chapter 7.

8.   See Chapter 8.

9.   See Chapter 6.

10.   As my academic teacher Wolfgang Ritzel put it: "The *aim of education* is to *convey autonomy* to those who are not of age. This aim of the practice of education functions as the principle of *educational theory*—the aim of which, in turn, is *understanding and true knowledge of education*" (Ritzel, 1980, p. 279).

11.   I refer to Klafki here instead of many others as his work—particularly his "Didactic Analysis" (1995; first published in 1958)—was very influential in German Didaktik in the 1960s and 1970s.

12.   See Chapter 3 for more details.

13.   There is a German equivalent of the English adjective "didactic" in this sense, *schulmeisterlich*.

14.   What I will not be considering in the following pages are all those issues, approaches, or even paradigms, that characterize German didactical discourse: "human-science," "communicative," "critical," or "*bildungstheoretische*" Didaktik, the "Berlin," the "Hamburg," or the "Marburg Didaktik." I will simply begin with the classroom.

15.   To be fair, I ought to point out that there are many mediating positions, some of which I will mention later on.

16.   Comenius was famous particularly because of his textbook, which mention in more detail in Chapters 4 and 9.

17.   Others were far more important for the professonalization of teaching, though; namely his successor, the classical scholar Friedrich August Wolf (1759–1824) as far as higher education is concerned, and Adolph Diesterweg (1790–1866) who had been more influential in the training of elementary teachers.

18.   This is an artificial term well known in the Eurpean discourse on education at the beginning of the 20th century. In the same sense as "psycho-logy" has the logic of "psyche" (mind) as its object, "pedo-logy" has "pais" (Greek: the child—etymologically hidden in *ped*agogic, too) as its object. The irritating label was to indicate some subtle differences between this approach and the "child-studies."

19.   I remember quite well that we all had to buy the German translation of Gage's *Handbook* and learn our lesson in research methods from "Kerlinger."

20.   Schleiermacher was a theologian by profession. He also gave lectures on education and its theory. Schleiermacher and Johann Friedrich Herbart (1776–1841) are regarded as the founders of educational theory in Germany.

21.   By the way, he edited Schleiermacher's lectures.

22. There is, of course, room for a whole body of nuances, restrictions, and extensions, which can be disregarded here.

23. Throughout this book, I speak of Didaktik when referring to German *Didaktik*. With "didactics," I mean the body of knowledge that deals with the classroom—which is more than a compendium of advices how to teach.

24. I have developed this concept in more detail in Menck (1975).

25. Picht said that with particular regard to the tripartite German school system which consisted (and in a way still consists) of three parallel school types at the secondary level: *Gymnasium, Realschule*, and *Hauptschule*. It is impossible to translate these terms without describing the German school system in detail, but let me say only this: The *Gymnasium* corresponds to the English grammar school and students have to choose between the schools at the age of 10, usually in accordance with their academic achievements at the primary school.

26. I should add that in the 1970s and 1980s, teacher training was reorganized along the lines of that discussion.

27. The term is also used in another way. It goes back to an even older usage, namely the adjectiv *"didaktike,"* which has to be completed by the noun *"techne"*: *"didaktike techne"*—to be translated as the art of teaching. This is the way Wolfgang Ratke translated it, and this understanding mostly underlies today's German Didaktik. I do not follow this usage.

28. At this point I have to add a remark on the meaning of the German term *Unterricht,* which cannot be simply translated into other languages. For English, the words "instruction" and "teaching" present themselves and are commonly used. But "instruction" as well as "teaching" focuses on the teachers' activity whereas when we speak of or write about *Unterricht,* we mean the process as a whole. So, following the usage of Bellack and others in the title of their famous book *The Language of the Classroom* (1966), I prefer to translate "classroom" or "classroom work" as translations of *Unterricht.*

29. *"Unterrichten und Lernen in der Schule"* (Teaching and Learning at School)—this is what one of the latest "Introductions to Didactics" (Wiater, 1993) is called. And the book *Didaktisches Denken* (Thinking Didactically) by Jürgen Diederich (1988) begins, for example, with a chapter about "Learning and its Limits" (*Das Lernen und seine Grenzen*). This contrasts sharply with the practical imperative of *Reform pädagogik* where only the child has to be at the center of attention. I do not want to reinforce this idea of child-centeredness, most especially, as a standard of "pedagogical correctness."

30. "Students" are not "human beings"—that is what I have noted down as a proposition for my students. Understandably they were a little startled.

31. Conditions such as these have been and are there whenever we talk about arkana and their tradition; during the education of groups and individuals respectively, which in principle differ from all the other members of society in their knowledge; noble education, education of the new generation of priests; one may also include the traditional training as a manual craftsman.

32. This label alludes to Georg Philipp Harsdörffer's *Poetischer Trichter* (poetical funnel) as a joke for a teaching method by which something can be drummed even into the most stupid minds.

33. Here and in the following pages, I refer to a reprint of the first—a Latin–German—edition of the *Orbis Pictus.*

34. The following is partly taken from Menck (1999; pp. 221–229).

35.   For *Weltbild*, see Chapter 9.

36.   This chapter is based on my book *Unterrichtsinhalt* (Content or an Essay on the Pedagogical Construction of Reality in the Classroom; 1986).

37.   N.B. When I speak of "Didaktik" I refer to the German Didaktik tradition as I have done up to this point.

38.   N is an abbreviation for "natural numbers"; that is, for the positive integers.

39.   It is really as a preparation for introducing "fractions" that the concept of the "divisor" is introduced in these lessons.

40.   See, for example, Menck (1989).

41.   It is the teacher who can see to it that not only the saints but also the heretics, not only the heroes but also the cowards and murderers, not only art but also kitsch finds its way into the classroom. I would like to recall this, just in case we forget that these, too, are what constitute humankind. By this I do not, of course, wish to propose that pupils should cultivate the potential murderer within themselves, but it would be good if they were able to recognize the potential murderer lurking within—and deal with this in a dignified, appropriate—in brief, in a humane—manner.

42.   I understand "interpretation" as work in which the elements of a text (in the broadest sense of the word) are juxtaposed with other elements, and with contextual elements, in such a way that they are meaningful for those participating.

43.   This is meant as an allusion to Berger and Luckmann (1966).

44.   See Menck (1986) for more details.

45.   For another example see Menck (1986). I wish to thank Marita Appoltshauser who videotaped the lessons together with Georg Wierichs and who proposed a first interpretation: *Praktisches und kommunikatives Handeln im Kunstunterricht*. Unpublished diplomarbeit, University of Siegen, 1982.

46.   So, for example, Bellack, Kliebard, Hyman, and Smith (1966).

47.   As, for example, Young (1971).

48.   For details, see Menck (1986).

49.   Martin et al. (1976); I refer here to this chapter in general without giving the page in every case.

50.   I here refer to Berger and Luckmann (1966).

51.   So, Bellack and colleagues (1966) did not ask the question, "What is international economics?" in the 15 lessons they had examined.

52.   Let me make another observation. It was also in the 1980s that teachers, and even politicians, became passionately interested in Lawrence Kohlberg's (1995) version of the problem of moral education—a version based on developmental psychology. I will not deal with this issue here. A sound knowledge of the moral development of children and adolescents is absolutely necessary for its formation. But this is not my central point of interest. First of all, it is essential to be fully aware of the *didactical* nature of the problem.

53.   My parents' *"das gehört sich nicht"* (you mustn't do that) or the French *"on fait"* (you have to do—in the sense of *"dos* and don'ts") are deeply rooted in my mind as the terms that indicate the consensus of what is to be done—a consensus that works the better the more tacit it is.

54.   It was not really my primer but it could have been: 1941 was the year I learned the numbers in the first grade of elementary school.

55.   The story goes back to the situation in which this chapter was presented first: to a seminar organized by members of the "Didaktik meets Curriculum" group and held in Oslo

in summer 1995. The parents of Susanne and Alexander *sailed* to Oslo to attend that seminar.

56.   Schola *est officina, in qua novelli animi ad Virtutem formantur.*

57.   *Nous avons donc cru qu'il importait d'avoir un Dictionnaire qu'on pût consulter sur toutes les matières des arts et des sciences, et qui servît autant à guider ceux qui se sentent le courage de travailler à l'instruction des autres, qu'à éclairer ceux qui ne s'instruisent que pour eux-mêmes* (d'Alembert, 1955 [1751], p. 194).

D'ou [c'est-à-dire du "Discours préliminaire," author's note] *nous inférons ... qu'il [son Dictionnaire] contribuera à la certitude, et au progrès des connaissances humaines; et qu'en multipliant le nombre des vrais savants, des artistes distingués et des amateur éclairés, il répandra dans la société des nouveaux avantages* (p. 232).

58.   The *Orbis Sensualium Pictus* was first published in a Latin–German version. Soon after an edition appeared in Czech—Comenius's mother tongue. I quote from a reprint of the Latin–German version (1978).

59.   Leis-Schindler (1991) and Hornstein (1997) have subtly analyzed the philosophy underlying the *Orbis Sensualium Pictus.*

60.   This picture is iconographically an exact equivalent to the last picture in Comenius's *Orbis.*

61.   Basedow was a Danish subject by birth. And it was in Anhalt-Dessau, one of the small German principalities, that he founded his reform school, the Philanthropin and that he worked out the *Elementarwerk.*

62.   The "loss of an objective order" is a *topos*, a commonplace in the discourse on education since Bollnow's time.

References

Adorno, T. W. (1972). Theorie der Halbbildung. In *Soziologische Schriften I* (pp. 93–121). Frankfurt: Europäische Verlagsanstalt.

Alt, R. (1960). *Bilderatlas zur Schul- und Erziehungsgeschichte. Band 1. Von der Urgesellschaft bis zum Vorabend der bürgerlichen Revolution.* Berlin: Volk und Wissen.

Alt, R. (1987). Herkunft und Bedeutung des "Orbis Pictus"—Ein Beitrag zur Geschichte des Lehrbuchs. In R. Alt, (Ed.), *Pädagogische Werke. Band. 2. Bearbeitet von R. Schulz* (pp. 183-222). Berlin: Volk und Wissen.

Amidon, E. J., & Hough, J. B. (Eds.). (1967). *Interaction analysis: Theory, research and application.* Reading, MA: Addison-Wesley.

Basedow, J. B. (1909). *J. B. Basedow's Elementarwerk mit den Kupfertafeln Chodowieckis u. a. Kritische Bearbeitung in drei Bänden* (T. Fritzsch, Ed.), Dritter Band. Leipzig: Ernst Weigandt. (Original work published 1787)

Basedow, J. B. (1965) *Ausgewählte pädagogische Schriften* (A. Reble, Ed.). Paderborn: Schöningh.

Bellack, A. A., Kliebard, H. M., Hyman, R. T., & Smith, F. L. (1966). *The language of the classroom.* New York: Teachers College Press.

Berger, P. L., & Luckmann, T. (1966). *The social construction of reality.* Garden City, NY: Doubleday.

Bernstein, B. (1975). On the classification and framing of educational knowledge. In B. Bernstein, (Ed.), *Class, Codes and Control 3. Towards a Theory of Educational Transmission.* London: Routledge and Kegan Paul, Ltd.

Bernstein, B. (1977). *Beiträge zu einer Theorie des pädagogischen Prozesses.* Frankfurt: Suhrkamp.

Blankertz, H. (1968). Bildungsbegriff. In I. Dahmer, & W. Klafki, (Eds.), *Geisteswissenschaftliche Pädagogik am Ausgang ihrer Epoche—Erich Weniger* (pp. 103-113). Weinheim, Berlin: Beltz.

Blankertz, H. (1969). *Theorien und Modelle der Didaktik.* München: Juventa.

Bollnow, O. F. (1960). Comenius und Basedow. *Sammlung, 15,* 141–153.

Bourdieu, P., & Passeron, J.-C. (1973). *Grundlagen einer Theorie der symbolischen Gewalt.* Frankfurt: Suhrkamp.

131

132 REFERENCES

Büttner, Rose, & Teichmann. (1937). *Rechenbuch für Hessen. Heft 1.* Ferdinand Hirt und Sohn.
Cassirer, E. (1956). *Wesen und Wirkung des Symbolbegriffs.* Darmstadt: Wissenschaftliche Buchgesellschaft.
Comenius, J. A. (1978) *Orbis sensualium pictus.* Dortmund: Harenberg Kommunikation. (Original work published 1658).
D'Alembert, J. L. (1955). *Discours Préliminaire de l'Encyclopédie* (E. Köhler, Ed.). Hamburg: Meiner.
Depaepe, M. (1993). *Zum Wohl des Kindes? Pädologie, pädagogische Psychologie und experimentelle Pädagogik in Europa und den USA, 1890–1940.* Weinheim: Beltz.
Derbolav, J. (1957) *Das "Exemplarische" im Bildungsraum des Gymnasiums. Versuch einer pädagogischen Ortsbestimmung des exemplarischen Lernens.* Düsseldorf: Schwann.
Derbolav, J. (1960). Versuch einer wissenschaftstheoretischen Grundlegung der Didaktik. *Zeitschrift für Pädagogik, 2. Beiheft* (pp. 17–45). Weinheim: Beltz.
Dewey, J. (1916). *Democracy and education.* New York: Macmillan.
Diderot, D. (1969) *Enzyklopädie. Philosophische und politische Texte aus der "Encyclopédie" sowie Prospekt und Ankündigung der letzten Bände.* München: Deutsches Taschenbuch Verlag.
Diederich, J. (1988). *Didaktisches Denken: Eine Einführung in Anspruch, Möglichkeiten und Grenzen der allgemeinen Didaktik.* Weinheim: Juventa.
Diesterweg, F. A. W. (1958) *Wegweiser zur Bildung für deutsche Lehrer* (J. Scheveling, Ed.). Paderborn: Schöningh.
Eisenlohr, M. F. (1992). *Deutsches Lesebüchlein.* Donauwörth: Auer. (Original work published 1920).
Flitner, W. (1958). *Das Selbstverständnis der Erziehungswissenschaft in der Gegenwart* (2nd ed). Heidelberg: Quelle und Meyer.
Grimsehl. (1950). Grimsehls Lehrbuch der Physik für höhere Lehranstalten. Teil 2. Neubearbeitet von W. German, W. Klieforth, & G. Schumm. Stuttgart, Mainz: Klett & Verlag für Technik und Wirtschaft.
Gundem, B. B. (1998). *Understanding European didactics—An overview: Didactics (Didaktik, didaktik(k), didactique.* (Report No. 4, 1998). Oslo: University of Oslo, Institute of Educational Research.
Gundem, B., & Hopmann, S. (1998) *Didaktik and/or Curriculum.* New York: Lang.
Hameyer, U. (1990). Lehr- und Lernforschung bis zum Jahr 2000: Wisssenssynthese als Förderungsschwerpunkt. *Unterrichtswissenschaft, 18,* 23–28.
Heimann, P. (1970). Didaktik als Theorie und Lehre. In D. C. Kochan, (Ed.), *Allgemeine Didaktik. Fachdidaktik. Fachwissenschaft. Ausgewählte Beiträge aus den Jahren 1953–1969* (pp. 110–142). Darmstadt: Wissenschaftliche Buchgesellschaft.
Henningsen, J. (1974). *Erfolgreich manipulieren. Methoden des Beybringens.* Ratingen: Henn.
Herbart, J. F. (1964). Über die ästhetische Darstellung der Welt als das Hauptgeschäft der Erziehung. In W. Asmus (Ed.), *Johann Friedrich Herbart. Pädagogische Schriften, Band 1* (pp. 105-121) (Original work published 1804). Düsseldorf, München: Küpper vorm. Bondi.
Hopmann, S., & Riquarts, K. (1995). *Didaktik and/or Curriculum.* Kiel: IPN.

Hornstein, H. (1997). *Die Dinge sehen, wie sie aus sich selber sind. Überlegungen zum Orbis pictus des Comenius*. Hohengehren: Schneider.

Humboldt, W. von (1960). Theorie der Bildung des Menschen. In A. Flitner & K. Giel (Eds.), *Gesammelte Schriften*, Band. I (pp. 234–240). Darmstadt: Wissenschaftliche Buchgesellschaft.

Husén, T., & Postlethwaite, T. N. (Eds.). (1994). *International encyclopedia of education* (2nd ed.). Oxford: Pergamon.

Keatinge, M. W. (1931). *Comenius*. New York: McGraw-Hill.

Key, E. (1900). *Das Jahrhundert des Kindes*. Berlin: Fischer.

Kirsch, A. (1976). Aspects of simplification in mathematics teaching. In H. Athen & H. Kunle (Eds.), *Proceedings of the Third International Congress on Mathematical Education* (pp. 98–120). Karlsruhe: International Congress on Mathematical Education.

Kirsch, A. (2000). Aspects of simplification in mathematics teaching. In I. Westbury, S. Hopmann, & K. Riquarts (Eds.), *Teaching as a reflective practice: The German Didaktik tradition* (pp. 267–284). Mahwah, NJ: Lawrence Erlbaum Associates.

Klafki, W. (1962). *Studien zur Bildungstheorie und Didaktik*. Weinheim: Beltz.

Klafki, W. (1964). *Das pädagogische Problem des Elementaren und die Theorie der kategorialen Bildung* (3rd/4th eds.). Weinheim: Beltz.

Klafki, W. (1985). *Neue Studien zur Bildungstheorie und Didaktik*. Weinheim, Basel: Beltz.

Klafki, W. (1995). Didactic analysis as the core of preparation of intruction [Didaktische Analyse als Kern der Unterrichtsvorbereitung]. *Journal of Curriculum Studies, 27*, 13–30.

Kohlberg, L. (1995). *Die Psychologie der Moralentwicklung*. Frankfurt: Suhrkamp.

Krathwohl, D., Bloom, B. S., & Masia, B. (1964). *A taxonomy of educational objectives. Handbook II. The affective domain*. New York: McKay.

Künzli, R. (2000). German Didaktik: Models of re-presentation, of intercourse, and of experience. In I. Westbury, S. Hopmann, & K. Riquarts (Eds.), *Teaching as a reflective practice: The German Didaktik tradition*. (pp. 41–54). Mahwah, NJ: Lawrence Erlbaum Associates.

Lay, W. (1908). *Experimentelle Didaktik. Ihre Grundlegung mit besonderer Rücksicht auf die Erziehung durch die Tat*. Liepzig: Teubner.

Leis-Schindler, I. (1991). Ding, Sprache, Anschauung und Bild im "Orbis pictus" des Johann Amos Comenius. In C. Rittelmeyer, & E. Wiersing, (Eds.), *Bild und Bildung. Ikonologische Interpretationen vormoderner Dokumente von Erziehung und Bildung* (pp. 215–236). Wiesbaden: Harrassowitz.

Luther, M. (1925). Deutsche Messe. In O. Clemen (Ed.), *Werke in Auswahl* Band. 3 (pp. 294–309). Bonn: Marcus und Weber.

Luther, M. (1925). Von der Freiheit eines Christenmenschen. In O. Clemen (Ed.), *Werke in Auswahl,* Band 2 (pp. 1–27). Bonn: Marcus und Weber.

Martin, N., Williams, P., Wilding, J., Hemmings, S., & Medway, P. (Eds.). (1976). *Understanding children talking*. London: Penguin Books.

Marx, K. (1953). *Die Frühschriften* (S. Landshut, Ed.). Stuttgart: Kröner.

Menck, P. (1975). *Unterrichtsanalyse und didaktische Konstruktion. Studien zur Theorie des Lehrplans und des Unterrichts*. Frankfurt: Fischer-Atenäum.

Menck, P. (1978). Some remarks on subject matter. In E. Komulainen & M. Koskenniemi, (Eds.), *Research in teaching* (Research Bulletin No. 49, pp. 114–128). University of Helsinki, Institute of Education.

Menck, P. (1980) Der Gegenstand alltäglichen Unterrichts. In D. Lenzen (Ed.), *Pädagogik und Alltag* (pp. 113–124). Stuttgart: Klett-Cotta.

Menck, P. (1983). Lehrplanreform und ihre Theorie. *Siegener Hochschulblätter, 6,* 1, 45–54.

Menck, P. (1986). *Unterrichtsinhalt oder: Ein Versuch über die Konstruktion der Wirklichkeit im Unterricht.* Frankfurt: Peter Lang.

Menck, P. (1987). Lehrplanarbeit nach Robinsohn. Beobachtungen aus Anlass einer Befragung. *Zeitschrift für Pädagogik, 33,* 363–380.

Menck, P.(1987). Throwing two dice: The content of a math lesson. *Journal of Curriculum Studies, 19,* 219–225.

Menck, P.(1989). Curriculum development in the Federal Republic of Germany—tradition or reform? *Education, 40,* 49–63.

Menck, P. (1995). Didactics as construction of content. *Journal of Curriculum Studies, 27,* 353–371.

Menck, P.(1999). *Geschichte der Erziehung* (2nd ed.). Donauwörth: Auer.

Meumann, E. (1914). Abriss der experimentellen Pädagogik. Leipzig: Wilhelm Engelmann.

Meyer, H. L. (1980). *Leitfaden zur Unterrichtsvorbereitung.* Königstein: Sciptor.

Michael, B., & Schepp, H. H. (1973). *Politik und Schule von der französischen Revolution bis zur Gegenwart,* Band 1. Frankfurt: Athenäum Fischer.

Nebe, A. (Ed.). (1927). *Eine Katechese August Hermann Franckes. Gehalten im August 1699.* Halle: Buchhandlung des Waisenhauses.

Otto, B. (1907). *Geistiger Verkehr mit Schülern im Gesamtunterricht. Unterrichtsprotokolle.* Grosslichterfelde: Verlag des Hauslehrers.

Petersen, P. (1965). *Die Pädagogische Tatsachenforschung* (T. Rutt, Ed.). Paderborn: Schöningh.

Picht, G. (1964). *Die deutsche Bildungskatastrophe.* Olten/Freiburg: Walter.

Ritzel, W. (1980). *Philosophie und Pädagogik im 20. Jahrhundert.* Darmstadt: Wissenschaftliche Buchgesellschaft.

Robinsohn, S. B. (1967). *Bildungsreform als Revision des Curriculum.* Neuwied: Luchterhand.

Rumpf, H. (1969). Sachneutrale Unterrichtsbeobachtung? *Zeitschrift für Pädagogik, 15,* 293–314.

Schleiermacher, F. D. E. (1966). *Friedrich Schleiermacher. Pädagogische Schriften. Erster Band. Die Vorlesungen aus dem Jahre 1826* (E. Weniger & T. Schulze, Eds.). Düsseldorf, München: Küpper vorm. Bondi.

Sinclair, J. M, & Coulthard, M. (1975). *Towards an analysis of discourse.* London: Oxford University Press.

Trapp, E. C. (1977). *Versuch einer Pädagogik* (U. Herrmann, Ed.). Paderborn: Schöningh.

von Hentig, H. (1994). *Die Schule neu denken.* München: Hanser.

Weniger, E. (1952). *Didaktik als Bildungslehre. Teil 1. Theorie der Bildungsinhalte und des Lehrplans.* Weinheim: Beltz.

Weniger, E. (1957). *Die Eigenständigkeit der Erziehung in Theorie und Praxis.* Weinheim: Beltz.

Weniger, E. (2000). Didaktik as a theory of education. In I. Westbury, S. Hopmann, & K. Riquarts (Eds.), *Teaching as a reflective practice: The German Didaktik tradition* (pp. 111–125). Mahwah, NJ: Lawrence Erlbaum Associates.

Wiater, W. (1993). Unterrichten und Lernen in der Schule. Eine Einführung in die Didaktik. Donauwörth: Auer.

Wittmann, H. (1941). *Von Drinnen und Draußen. Ein Lesebuch für die Kleinen.* Frankfurt am Main: Verlag Moritz Diesterweg.

Witz, K. G. (2000). The "academic problem." *Journal of Curriculum Studies, 32* (1), 9–23.

Young, M.F.D. (1971). *Knowledge and control. New directions for the sociology of knowledge.* London: Collier-Macmillan.

Author Index

A

Adorno, T. W., 75, *131*
Alt, R., 44, *131*
Amidon, E. J., 9, *131*

B

Basedow, J. B., 48, 105, 118, 119, 120, *131*
Bellack, A. A., 71, 76, 127n, 128n, *131*
Berger, P. L., 128n, *131*
Bernstein, B., 62, *131*
Blankertz, H., 22, 98, *131*
Bloom, B. S., 99, *133*
Bollnow, O. F., 121, 123, *131*
Bourdieu, P., 27, *131*
Büttner, 104, *132*

C

Cassirer, E., 75, *132*
Comenius, J. A., 45, 74, 102, 103, 109, 113, 114, 115, 116, 117, 129, *132*
Coulthard, M., 72, 73, *134*

D

D'Alembert, J. L., 129n, *132*
Depaepe, M., 6, 8, *132*
Derbolav, J., 97, 105, *132*
Dewey, J., 126n, *132*

Diderot, D., 112, *132*
Diederich, J., 127n, *132*
Diesterweg, F. A. W., 20, *132*

E

Eisenlohr, M. F., 103, *132*

F

Flitner, W., 2, *132*

G

Grimsehl, 36, *132*
Gundem, B. B., xiii, 125n, *132*

H

Hameyer, U., 9, *132*
Heimann, P., 21, 98, *132*
Hemmings, S., 17, 128n, *133*
Henningsen, J., 42, 43, *132*
Herbart, J. F., 106, 107, *132*
Hopmann, S., 5, 125n, *132*
Hornstein, H., 129n, *133*
Hough, J. B., 9, *131*
Humboldt, W., von, 12, *133*
Husén, T., 125n, *133*
Hyman, R. T., 71, 76, 128n, *131*

K

Keatinge, M. W., 19, *133*
Key, E., 122, *133*

Kirsch, A., xi, *133*
Klafki, W., 2, 16, 21, 55, 74, 99, 100, 125n, *133*
Kliebard, H. M., 71, 76, 128n, *131*
Kohlberg, L., 128n, *133*
Komensky *see* Comenius
Krathwohl, D., 99, *133*
Künzli, R., xv, *133*

L
Lay, W., 6, *133*
Leis-Schindler, I., 129n, *133*
Luckmann, T., 128n, *131*
Luther, M., 43, 46, *133*

M
Martin, N., 17, 128n, *133*
Marx, K., 12, 13, 27, *133*
Masia, B., 99, *133*
Medway, P., 17, 128n, *133*
Menck, P., 84, 127n, 128n, *133, 134*
Meumann, E., 6, *134*
Meyer, H. L., 77, 100, 101, *133, 134*
Michael, B., 43, *134*

N
Nebe, A., 46, *134*

O
Otto, B., 50, *134*

P
Passeron, J.-C., 27, 60, *131*
Petersen, P., 8, 9, *134*

Picht, G., 21, *134*
Postlethwaite, T. N., 125n, *133*

R
Riquarts, K., 5, 125n, *132*
Ritzel, W., 126n, *134*
Robinsohn, S. B., 21, *134*
Rose, 104, *132*
Rumpf, H., 55, *134*

S
Schepp, H. H., 43, *134*
Schleiermacher, F. D. E., 6, *134*
Sinclair, J. M., 72, 73, *134*
Smith, F. L., 71, 76, 128n, *131*

T
Teichmann, 104, *132*
Trapp, E. C., 5, *134*

V
von Hentig, H., 98, *134*

W
Weniger, E., xv, 7, 15, 28, *134, 135*
Westbury, I., 125n,
Wiater, W., 127n, *135*
Wilding, J., 17, 128n, *133*
Williams, P., 17, 128n, *133*
Wittmann, H., 105, 108, *135*
Witz, K. G., xiv, *135*

Y
Young, M. F. D., 128n, *135*

Subject Index

A

acquisition, 52
adolescents *see* youth
Adorno, 75
affective domain, 99
alienation, 62
Allgemeinbildung
   allgemeine Bildung, xiv, 15
   see also education, general
art lesson, education, xvi, 78–85
articulation, 33
authority, 32, 68
autonomy
   autonomous subject, 3, 5, 61, 89,
      96, 126. *See also* self-deter-
      mination, maturity
   relative, of the educational system,
      68
axiom of a theory of Unterricht, 23,
     24, 35, 38, 39

B

Bild *see* picture
Bildung, xiv, xix, 11–13, 15–18, 31,
     53, 69, 74, 75, 77, 86, 107,
     111–113, 122, 123, 125. *See
     also* formation, theory of, xi–
     xiv, 13, 30

Bildungsgehalt, 15
Bildungsinhalt, 15
Bildungskatastrophe, 21
Bildungsprozess, 37
Bohemian Brethren, 43–45, 118
bourgeois, 45, 118, 119, 121

C

catechetical method, 46–49
catechism, 45, 46
child-centered, 25, 32
Chodowiecki, 119, 121
classroom, xiv, 23, 37, 58, 77, 93, 96,
     106
   discourse, 71, 73
   practice, 7, 22
   process, 3, 34
   research, 6, 9, 55, 94
   situation, vi
   theory of, 6, 33, 40. *See also* theory
     of teaching
   work, xvi, 16, 21–24, 29, 33, 35, 37,
     38, 62, 63, 69, 83, 89, 107,
     109, 110, 125
commitment, 52, 99, 100
conscience, 38, 95–97, 107, 117, 121
   formation of the, xvii, xviii, 96, 101,
     102, 105, 106
consensus, 105, 110

content of classroom, instruction, teaching, 55–58, 62, 69, 72, 74, 77, 78, 87
cultural minimum, 14, 24
culture, 13, 25, 26, 27, 35, 38, 39, 75
  passing on of, 23
  ruling–oppressed, 28
curriculum, 14, 22
  theory, research, xii, 28, 60, 61, 68

D

Didactic analysis, 16, 21, 55, 74
didactic indicative, 97–99
Didactica magna (Great Didactic), 2, 5, 19, 20, 45. *See also* Comenius
didactical
  context, field, 92, 98
  discourse, 1, 13, 14
  framing, purpose, 113, 119
  inventions, 50
  logic, 73, 76
  maxim, 92
  preparation, 64. *See also* lesson planning
  principles, 40
  reduction, 28
  reflection, 102
  reasoning, 13, 14, 18
  theory, 4, 7. *See also* teaching, theory of
  triangle, 25, 57
didactician, 4, 38, 109
didactics, 3, 4, 7, 13, 23, 38, 40, 75, 127
Didaktik, xi, xiii, xvii, xvii, 3, 6, 12, 20–23, 33, 40, 55–57, 59, 61, 62, 74, 86, 95, 96, 98, 125, 127
  Bildung-centered, xi, xiv–xvi
  see also human-science concept of Didaktik
Didaktik meets Curriculum, vii, xi, 128

Dilthey, xii
discipline, problem of, 62, 65, 68
  school, 13–15, 39, 62

E

education, 24, 52, 53, 59, 62, 89, 96, 99, 112, 126
  compensatory, 28
  for all, general, 14, 31, 43. *See also* Allgemeinbildung
  history of, 52, 61
educational
  objectives, 22, 98, 99, 101, 102
  policy, 68
  politics, 52, 59
  research, 2, 4, 6, 8–10, 21, 51, 55, 94. *See also* educational theory; research in education
  theory, xii–xiv, xvii, 6, 51, 126. *See also* educational research
educator, 32
Elementarwerk, 48, 105, 111, 112, 118–122
Encyclopédie, 113
enkyklios paideia, 15
Enlightenment, enlighten(ed), xiv, 53, 112, 122
ethnomethodologist, 1, 93
everyday
  life, 29, 37, 39, 57, 61, 89, 103, 104, 107, 109, 113
  situations, 29, 73, 103, 110
experience(s)
  teachers', 4
  students', 61

F

Fachdidaktik, xiii, 15. *See also* subject matter
formation, xiv, xvi, 17, 109, 125. *See also* Bildung

G

Geisteswissenschaft(liche Päda-
    gogik), xii, xiii, xv
generation, older, younger, 6, 24–26,
    28, 32, 39
German
    education, school system, 21, 68,
        127
    tradition, xii, 20
    educational thinking, theory, xii,
        xiii
    see also Didaktik
good
    the, xviii, 106
    (and bad), 102, 105, 106, 109, 121,
        123
grouping of students, 31
guidelines, 66
Gymnasium, 12, 107

H

hands-on learning, -activity, 76, 77,
    100
Hegel, 75
human achievement, xiv, xvi, 61
    being, humans, 12, 13, 26, 29, 31,
        32, 112. *See also* humane,
        humankind
    opportunities, 60
    spirit, 27
humane, 14, 38, 60, 128
humanity, xiv, 12, 14, 69, 76
humankind, xvii, 13, 14, 27, 61, 89,
    116, 128

I

iconographic(al), 116, 121, 128
initiation rites, 12
informing, 33. *See also* teaching
institution, 23
interpretation of symbols, 37, 59, 77
interest groups, 15

K

Kant, 112
knowledge, 38, 60, 89, 97, 107, 109,
    117, 121, 123
    passing on of, 3, 96
    production genesis of, 59, 61
    professional, of teachers, 20
    school, 60, 68, 75
    validity of, 93

L

learning activity, 76
Lehrerseminar, 20
Lehrplan, xvi, 22, 66, 76, 125. *See also*
    curriculum, guidelines
Lehrplantheorie, xvi, 59, 60, 76. *See
    also* curriculum theory
lesson planning, preparation, 10, 33,
    55, 84
life world, 57, 61, 107
life, 37, 89, 93. *See also* everyday life

M

mathematics, 64, 67, 68, 88, 90
    teaching, lesson, xvi, 63–69, 87–93
matter *see* subject matter
maturity, 97. *See also* autonomy
mediation, 60
method (of teaching), methodically,
    33, 42, 46, 52, 106, 119
models of Didaktik, didactical, 3, 4,
    21, 22, 56
moral, morality, 102, 103, 106, 121,
    128
Müller-Petersen, 9

N

nature, 5, 26, 27
needs
    of students, 30, 40
    subjective—objective, 31

of humankind, 27
Nürnberger Trichter, 35

O

objective orientation, 58
Orbis Pictus, 20, 45, 73, 103, 111–118,
    121–123
order, 116, 121, 122, 123
outcome of classroom work, 58, 61,
    62, 68

P

Pädagogik, xii, xiii
pädagogische Tatsachenforschung, 8
passing on of culture, 3, 23, 24, 32
pedagogical(ly),
    action, acting, 55, 68
    authority, 76, 89
    concern, 94
    institution, 77
    logic, xvi
    legitimation, 85, 86
    problem, 7
    process, 77
    purpose, 78
    reality, xviii
    situation, xviii, 8, 9, 40, 62, 78
personality, xiv, 106
Philanthropists, 7, 48, 49, 112, 119,
    121
picture(s) and story, -ies, xviii, xx, 45,
    53, 73, 75, 95, 101, 106, 107,
    109, 111, 116, 117, 119, 121,
    122
power, 51, 60, 68, 76
preparation of teaching see lesson
    planning
presentation, aesthetic, 110
primer, 103, 150, 123
profession(alization) of teaching, 5,
    20, 126
progressive, progressivism, xiii, xvii,
    37

pupil, see student

R

R's, the three, 14
Ratke, 1, 5
reality, pedagogically constructed, 78,
    86
reception of knowledge, 33, 35
recollection, teaching as, 35
Referendariat, internship, 85
reflection, engaged, xiii, 2
Reformpädagogen, reform peda-
    gogues, 49, 51, 52
Reformpädagogik, reform pedagogy,
    2, 62, 76
representation, see symbolic represen-
    tation
responsibility, 99–101
    pedagogical, 2

S

school, xvi, 66, 89
    elementary, 45
schooling, xvii, xix
selection from culture, 28, 29, 51, 59,
    76
self-activity, xiv
self-determination, 61. See also auton-
    omy
setting, of students, 66. See also
    grouping
social (societal) practice, 57, 59–61,
    75, 104, 105
society, 14, 23, 25, 26, 32, 39, 68, 121
Socrates, 35, 49, 51
story, -ies, see picture(s)
student, 26, 29–31
subject
    (matter), 25, 26, 32, 57, 58, 69, 75,
        76, 87, 94, 105
    (matter) didactics, 14, 15, 39
    see also Fachdidaktik
subjects, school, 57

symbol, 37
symbolic, 34, 35
    forms, 75
    representation, 59, 75, 86, 107, 113,
        117

T

tabula rasa, 35
teacher, 2, 26, 31, 32, 68, 76, 106
teacher education, formation, training,
        xii, 20, 53, 54, 98
teaching
    educative, 96
    theory of, reflection on, 23, 24, 98
    see also didactical theory
teaching profession, 20
textbook, 63, 111
    of Didaktik, 25, 40
theories
    of Didaktik, 56
tolerance, 96
topic of work in classroom, 14, 58, 62,
        68

U

Unterricht, 3, 125, 127
Unterrichtsinhalt *see* content of class-
        room
use and abuse, xviii, 102, 103, 117

W

Weltbild, xviii, xix, 16, 17, 32, 53, 61,
        111, 117, 118, 121, 122
work
    in society, 35, 36
    in classroom, 76, 109
    see also classroom work
world, real, outside, 86, 106, 112
world-view *see* Weltbild

Y

young *see* youth
youth, 30, 37, 39

DATE DUE

GAYLORD   #3522PI   Printed in USA